the girl butterfly tattoo

a girl's guide to claiming her power

Dannielle Miller

BANTAM

SYDNEY AUCKLAND TORONTO NEW YORK LONDON

A Bantam book
Published by Random House Australia Pty Ltd
Level 3, 100 Pacific Highway, North Sydney NSW 2060
www.randomhouse.com.au

First published by Bantam in 2012

Addresses for companies within the Random House Group can be found at
www.randomhouse.com.au/offices

National Library of Australia
Cataloguing-in-Publication Entry

Miller, Dannielle
The girl with the butterfly tattoo / Dannielle Miller

ISBN 978 1 74275 255 6 (pbk.)

Teenage girls.
Teenage girls – Life skills guides.

649.125

Cover image courtesy Getty Images
Cover design by Ciara Fulcher
Internal design and typeset by Post Pre-press Group
Printed in Australia by Griffin Press, an accredited ISO AS/NZS 14001:2004
Environmental Management System printer

For Teyah, Kye and Jaz. My darlings.

Contents

Introduction

> We delight in the beauty of the butterfly, but
> rarely admit the changes it has gone through to
> achieve that beauty.
>
> Maya Angelou

Traditionally butterflies have been used to symbolise change or transformation. I wholeheartedly believe that we are all able to change, that we can make choices and are in control. This is why I chose the butterfly as a symbol for my girl-power company, Enlighten Education.

Enlighten works with thousands of teen girls in schools right across Australia, New Zealand and Singapore every year (next stop, world domination! *insert evil laugh*). Rather than telling girls what to do, we focus on informing, inspiring and empowering them. We encourage girls to be discerning consumers and critical thinkers, and to find their own voice and power in a complex world. My job is a-maz-ing.

Another reason butterflies appeal to me is that while they appear to be gentle and are so pretty that they could almost be dismissed as merely decorative, in ancient times they were used to symbolise some much darker and more intriguing concepts.

The ancient Greeks used the same word, *psyche*, for the butterfly and the soul. Seems there might be some real depth to these girly-girls of the insect world. I'm loving that.

Ancient Greek mythology also tells us about my all-time favourite women warriors, the Amazons. These fierce women fought to protect their territory. Their weapons may have included the double-sided axe, which is butterfly shaped – nothing prissy here. One internet site I visited even suggested the Amazons went into battle holding up a staff emblazoned with a butterfly, symbolising that they, too, were beautiful and hard to capture. (And hey – if it's on the net it must be true, right?)

So whether the butterfly is a symbol for change, the soul or female fighting power, *I am all about the butterfly*.

The butterfly effect

I called my first book – which was aimed at women, particularly mums – *The Butterfly Effect*.

The idea of the butterfly effect comes from the science of chaos theory. It suggests that everything in this world is interconnected, so that the beating of a butterfly's wings in one part of the world may ultimately contribute to a tornado happening in another part of the world. Small changes can make a huge difference. I really believe this to be true.

This book, my second, is not designed to be a comprehensive 'guide for teen girls' that covers everything from puberty through to passing exams. I want to home in on the things that girls I meet every day in schools say make them *feel less* – less beautiful, less powerful, less happy, less in control. I want to help shift that self-doubt and clear up some of the confusion you may feel.

I know that if I can appeal to your head, hand and heart I will be able to help you make some small, yet very powerful, changes.

Your head
For your head, I will provide the facts.

Your hand
For your hand, you will find practical action plans and affirmations at the end of the chapters. Each action plan includes things you can do right now and long-term changes you can make to address the issues described in that chapter.

'intuitive' = known through direct insight, without being taught

The affirmations are short, positive statements you can use to boost your strength or chart a new course in your life. Some people find it helpful to repeat an affirmation when they wake each morning; others use them when the going gets tough.

Some like to write affirmations down and pin them up around the house. One mum sent me a picture of her bathroom mirror, on which she and her daughter write the affirmations each week so they are reminded to say them whenever they look at themselves. How cool is that?

Your heart

Most importantly, in this book I will appeal to your heart, by sharing my stories and those of the girls I have met along the way. I hope that the advice makes intuitive, emotional sense to you, as I believe that is the only kind of advice anyone should follow.

Always at the centre of my approach is love and laughter – and there is nothing soft or airy-fairy about this. Building positive emotions and healthy connections with other people makes us feel far healthier and more joyful. Research proves it.

So, if I am going to be expecting you to connect with me, I guess I better tell you a little more about myself – true?

Who am I?

Whenever I work with girls in schools, I ask them to complete an evaluation form afterwards. One of the questions is 'What did you think today would be like?' The answers usually run along the lines of 'I thought you'd be a boring old bag trying to tell us what we do wrong and what we need to do; no offence.' (BTW, don't you love it when people say something offensive and conclude with 'No offence'? *Why would I be offended just because you assumed I'd be old, and boring?*)

Truth is, I am not offended by comments like these, as I understand them. In fact, this type of feedback just makes me smile to myself. I so get where these girls are coming from. They are right. They do not need a big lecture from me. Nor do you. Yawnsville.

To help counter girls' preconceived ideas of me, one of the first things I do is tell them a bit more about me so they can understand that I do not see myself as some kind of perfect person, but as a woman who just genuinely thinks she can help put things in perspective.

Another reason I do this is that I used to hate it when I was at school and a teacher or guest speaker came in and asked us to think about our lives without sharing anything of themselves first. Quite possibly I was just a particularly nosy kid, but somehow that seemed really unfair.

So, what's my story?

Well, I guess if you took a snapshot of my life at the moment, I would look a little like this:

+ Mum to the world's most talented, delightful children (biased much?) – my daughter, Teyah (13); son, Kye (10); and stepdaughter, Jazmine (17).
+ Partner to a very sweet, funny man. He won me over by promising to make me Anzac biscuits and to always be excited to see me – how could I say no to a date with a guy like that?
+ Ex–high school teacher. I started my career teaching kids a little like Jonah from *Summer Heights High*. I loved them. I loved teaching. I love kids.
+ Co-founder and leader of a group of amazing women who run workshops for teen girls in schools. Enlighten Education spreads girl power to more than 20,000 teen girls a year across Australia and New Zealand. Giddy up.
+ Author of a book on raising confident, happy teen girls, *The Butterfly Effect*. (Funny story: I was once at a conference and a teen girl ran up to me and said, 'Oh my gosh, I loved the movie of your book!' Ummm . . . sorry, sweetheart but I am not pals with Ashton Kutcher.)
+ Blogger and self-confessed Facebook addict.
+ Regular guest on TV shows, including Channel 9's *Kerri-Anne*. (Highlight: I met The Wiggles backstage

recently. Kye was with me that day and instead of making Wiggly fingers, he inadvertently made pointy-gun fingers. Not so Wiggly, dude! What is it with little boys and shooting?)

- Fur-mummy to two dogs, Mia (border collie) and Lucy (cavoodle), and two bunnies, Fatsy and Charlotte (Kye named poor Fatsy).

- Big fan of Wonder Woman, friends who make a snorting sound when they giggle, ugg boots in winter, Red Tulip Easter bunnies, sniffing people (I love how my family and friends smell – is that weird?), books, feminism (it is not scary – promise – and maybe by the end of this book you'll embrace the 'f' word, too) and laughing so hard I think I may wet myself.

But none of that stuff about who I am now really helps you understand why this work matters to me so much. And it really does. So I am going to have to start at the very beginning . . .

1

The Battle Within

A young English girl who called herself 'Mememolly' started a phenomenon on YouTube when she posted 'something of an apologetic love letter' to her body. She listed parts of her body – her feet, arms, ears, eyes – and talked about why she appreciated them. A flood of people responded by posting their own video responses, telling the world how they feel about their bodies.

Inspired by them, on the morning that I turned 38, I sat down and wrote my own letter of thanks to my body:

Dear body,

I am really happy with the way we are growing old together.

Thanks, feet, for being so pretty. I love the way your nails look when they are painted. I haven't always treated you so well, though. I have stopped wearing killer heels quite so often, but hey, we both know the damage is done.

Thanks, legs. You are fabulous; you're so long and you rarely change shape, even when I eat loads of junky foods. You have made me feel glamorous on many occasions.

Belly – what can I say? You are a podgy, bloated little thing, aren't you? I have tried exercising you, sucking you in and constraining you in special 'Bridget Jones' style bloomers – but you just will not be denied.

Breasts – you will not be denied, either, but you are lovely. You make me feel so feminine. And you fed both my children; that was truly amazing. I will be forever grateful.

Arms. My special body parts. Lefty – you are a bit of a non-event really, aren't you? I don't write with you and you are quite nondescript. But righty – yes, you have tales to tell. I love your burn scars now. Really. I do. You make me strong, unique and show the world I am a girl with a history of bravery. I am sorry that I hid you for so many years when I was young, but I just hadn't learnt how to deal with something so large. We both had to grow into the tight, twisted and melted flesh.

Face – you are just fine. Elegantly shaped eyebrows, a few wrinkles that show I have lived, laughed and worried.

Hair – I am sorry I bleach you. You do well to hang in there – but I do treat you to great shampoos and head rubs from my girlfriends.

Thanks, body, for getting me this far. You are so resilient and so strong. You rarely get sick and you can withstand great pain. You are an Amazon's body.

Happy Birthday. xxxx

Scarred and scared

When I was two years old, I was badly burnt. I received third-degree burns all down my right arm and neck. As is often the case with burn victims, I also suffered two major secondary infections, German measles and the potentially life-threatening golden staph.

My great-grandmother burnt me. She poured hot cooking oil down on me as I sat watching breakfast being prepared. As a small girl, I was always told this was an accident, yet I questioned why no one ever spoke of this woman again, let alone saw her. *Why hadn't we forgiven her?* I wondered. After all, accidents do happen.

It was only when I was older that the truth emerged. Great Grandma had been unstable and had shown signs of violence towards my beloved grandmother when she was a small girl, too. Everyone felt instinctively that she had burnt me deliberately.

I don't remember whether it was done to me deliberately. Ultimately, as it cannot be undone, I have chosen not to focus on that question. It happened.

What do I remember? I remember my grandmother's face as she came through the doorway in response to my screams. I recall thinking I must be very badly hurt as she looked devastated.

I remember my doctor, too. As I was hospitalised for almost six months, he became a central figure in my life. He was kind, gentle and doting. I was his special girl. Heaven help any nurse who dared keep me waiting!

I remember gifts, in particular, books. Perhaps this was the start of my love affair with words. I loved being read to. I escaped pain and boredom through tales of princesses with power and adventures of other little girls who faced great dangers and emerged triumphant.

I soothed myself with words, too. I could not yet read, of course, but I would talk to myself when frightened, repeating over and over the mantra 'You'll be okay, you'll be all right.' It was my secret spell and I would cast it to give me strength.

How fortunate that these are my memories: of being loved, spoilt, protected and strong.

For my family, other, darker memories remain as well. Memories of me writhing in pain as my dressings were changed, of being told that my arm would need to be amputated, of being advised that I would need yet another skin graft, of being told time and time again that I would not live.

But live I did. And I kept my arm. With its red, raised, twisted flesh, it looked different to the arms of my friends. There was a flap of skin near my elbow that was taut when my arm was stretched out and hung loose when my arm was bent. Yet as a small child these differences did not concern me – I was so much more than my body!

I was a busy, bossy little girl. I had a younger sister to organise, lollies to eat, Barbies to collect and, once school started, more books to devour. In childhood, my body was merely an instrument to carry me from one adventure to the next. When I wanted to join my friends at the beach, I just had Mum cut the toes out of one of my father's socks and popped that on to protect my arm from the sun. Problem solved!

Hiding

Around the time I turned ten, things definitely changed. I started noticing boys. And I started noticing the girls the boys noticed. At school, the boys preferred the alpha girls: popular, pretty, often good at sport. I was a pretty enough girl and had a few close friends, but as I was more interested in reading than netball, I was definitely not alpha material. It wasn't just at school that I received messages about what defined beauty and sexual attractiveness. My Barbies, *Charlie's Angels*, ABBA – all of them taught me that to be a desired woman, I would need to be thin, beautiful and immaculately groomed. No scars allowed.

I entered adolescence and, like most girls, began a new internal conversation. I was no longer casting spells to heal myself. Instead, I was engaging in darker, self-destructive thoughts and telling myself that I was not enough. Not pretty enough, not thin enough, not popular enough. My feelings of inadequacy due to my scarring became quite overwhelming. I was still bright and ambitious but my main preoccupation was how best I could hide my scars from the world.

I hid. I hid my arm. I wore skivvies underneath my summer uniform, wore jumpers all year round. I avoided pools and beaches. My arm no longer seemed small; it seemed enormous. A huge, horrible, disfigured limb I would be forced to drag through what had been my oh-so-promising life.

Yes, teenage girls have always been good at drama.

I vividly recall my daydreams at age 15 about what my life would be like if I had not been burnt. I was tall and had very long legs, so I fancied that I could have been a bikini model if it had not been for my arm. For many girls it is not the actual job of being a model that appeals. It is the kudos, the knowledge that one's body has been declared special. Worthy of attention. 'If I looked that way, then they would love me . . .' Sound familiar?

At school, I hid my scars not only with the sleeves of my jumper but also by seeming self-assured. I knew that if I appeared vulnerable, I would be targeted. So I spent my free time joining in with other kids rating one another. I went to an all-girls school and at lunchtime it was as if the magazines we read, which told us what clothes were in and whether a celebrity was hot or not, had sprung to life. We may not have been able to control many elements of our lives, but we could definitely control one another through ridicule. The ratings we gave one another might not have been held up like scores in a talent show, but they were branded on our psyches.

The rules in girls' rating games were the same then as they are now. Be considered hot by others, in particular by boys, and you score points. Getting a highly desired boyfriend means an instant advance to the top of the club. I was lucky enough to land the school hottie from the boys' school next door and was elevated from classroom nerd to the girl everyone wanted to know, almost overnight.

He dumped me a year later for a girl considered hotter. At 14, she was a fashion model appearing in women's magazines and parading in women's designer labels. My dream run at the top of the charts was over. I had all my deepest fears confirmed. The prettiest girl did win. In my mind, the break-up was all about me not being beautiful enough. It seemed all the more tragic because I had elevated him to godlike status for loving me despite my scars.

Looking back, I see how ridiculous all this was. I was funny, bright, passionately in love with him. He was not doing me any favours by being with me!

It seems strange to me now that at no stage did I stop and think that perhaps my relationship with this boy had broken down for reasons other than my appearance. Possibly it had been the pressure of us getting too serious too soon (the reason my boyfriend gave me at the time) or maybe we were just growing apart. He may have just been a jerk. And the truth is, while the new girl certainly was beautiful, she may have been so much more than just her looks, too.

Healing

It was only when I became a teacher that I finally explored ways in which I might come to terms with my burns. If

I could not accept myself, how could I possibly ask my students to accept themselves?

I searched once again for soothing words, and found them in the writing of women such as Naomi Wolf, who wrote in *The Beauty Myth*: 'We don't need to change our bodies, we need to change the rules.' In women such as Sofia Loren: 'Nothing makes a woman more beautiful than the belief that she is beautiful.' And in the words of the young women I now taught: 'I love how you wear your scars, Miss, you don't let them wear you.' How amazing were my students?

Words healed me. And my self-talk once more became focused on my strengths rather than my perceived weaknesses. I *was* okay. It *would be* all right.

And everything was okay. And it was more than just all right. Life without self-doubt was magnificent. I loved and I was loved. As a confident 20-something, I shone.

I have a picture of me taken back then, when I went to the Amazon, in South America, for my honeymoon. It captures the authentic me. I look strong, fit. I am wearing a singlet top and grinning from ear to ear. I had been trekking in the jungle with my new husband and we had stumbled upon a village.

When the local children saw my burn scars they ran and hid from me. Our guide explained that they feared I would die soon, as they were not used to seeing large scars. In the Amazon, as there is no running water or electricity, if you get a major injury you will most likely die from infection. I assured our guide that he should tell the children I was fine. And one by one, they came across and touched my arm, played with my hair and started telling me in the local language that I was a strong, brave girl. A warrior girl.

Yes. I am an Amazon warrior. I am more than my body. It is such a small part of the entire Dannielle Miller story that it has again been relegated to a co-starring role. I have managed to move from hating my body to not just accepting it but loving it, scars and all. I don't think it is perfect, but I am okay with that. This is me.

Sometimes I choose to indulge in the trappings of conventional beauty, such as heels and hair dye. I do so knowing that these things may be fun, and they may make me feel pampered or be just what my outfit calls for on a special occasion, but they do not make me worth more or ensure I will be loved. I feel equally as valuable when I'm at home wearing my ugg boots and track pants, with my hair pulled back in an un-brushed mop.

And though I may get occasionally frustrated with my tummy, I cannot bring myself to hate it for a moment. It is part of me. My body is like a dear friend: not perfect, yet lovable and comforting, quirks and all. Despite what advertisers say, diets, surgery and cosmetics do not have some mystical power that will bring us eternal happiness. I know this.

How liberating! And, unfortunately, how rare. Many girls will not grow to be women who love their bodies. They will believe that if they just had the right-shaped breasts, or a flatter tummy, or a smaller nose, their life would be complete. They will bare scars of their own for many years – it's just that their scars may not be quite as obvious as mine.

◦◦◦

At war with our own bodies

Many girls are enslaved to their bodies. Their supposed imperfections – be they scars, weight or bust size – take on monstrous proportions. This deprives them of finding that Amazon power within. Statistics tell the story bluntly: 94 per cent of teenage girls wish, some of the time, that they were more beautiful. A quarter of teenage girls want to change everything physically about themselves.

The problem with statistics is that it is easy for us to be emotionally detached and for the numbers to become somewhat meaningless. But each number is a real girl. A girl who wakes up hungry and chooses to stay that way all day. A girl who is deeply sad. A girl who feels that she is unloved and unlovable. A girl who limps through her days hiding, through actual physical withdrawal, or by assuming an 'I am sooo fine' facade, or by ridiculing others to deflect attention away from herself. Living with a sense of inadequacy hurts. Occasionally this girl will take the ache from within her own chest and throw it at other girls, allowing herself just that little bit of breathing space. This girl might tease and belittle others, hoping that then no one will notice her own perceived flaws.

I have cried for, and with, many of the girls I have worked with, as they shared with me the pain of being at war with their own bodies.

> I have struggled since I was six with weight and body image . . . I haven't eaten for a week in an attempt to be beautiful.
>
> Katia, 15

> My whole life, I have been called just 'that fat kid'.
>
> Lucy, 14

> I think I am not as pretty as other girls. I hate the way I look, as it means I can't make friends.
>
> Samantha, 12

> I don't like to look in mirrors or get my photo taken, 'cause I am not beautiful. None of the girls I see in magazines look like me, because my skin is really dark. I wish I could make it whiter.
>
> Stephanie, 13

Often, I do not cry out of sadness. My workshops are incredibly joyful. I cry tears of joy and gratitude, too. I try to help heal and soothe and show girls that there is another way.

You *can* silence your inner critic and begin a new conversation within, a conversation that is affirming rather than destroying.

∼

The war waged on our bodies

If you are at war with your own body, you are far from alone. Many girls and women are sucked into the same body-hating vortex. Even us 'big girls' (your mother, teachers, aunties) tell you that you are beautiful the way you are, while we angst over our weight and wrinkles. Have you noticed that happening? It is not only hypocritical of us, it is sad, isn't it? Self-doubt is exhausting.

We all – girls and women – have to make this right. We have to move beyond this. If you already have, well done. If you are dealing with body issues, then let's attempt to shift things.

In my workshops, I ask girls to look at the source of their feelings of inadequacy about their bodies. Girls may have their own individual reasons for feeling uncomfortable with their appearance, such as experiences they had in the past. Body image is also shaped by social, political, racial, age and gender factors.

But there is something all girls and women share: we are at war with our bodies because there is a war being *waged on* our bodies. We are surrounded by words and images dictating what beauty is. The television shows we watch, the websites we browse, the music and radio stations we listen to, the newspapers and magazines we read – all of them bombard us with messages about what makes girls and women beautiful, desirable and worthy. Almost none of these messages offer a healing or empowering idea of feminine beauty.

Advertising is perhaps the worst offender. The average person sees around 75 ads every day. We see them on television, in newspapers and magazines, on the sides of buses, on our streets, when we are surfing the net and on the backs of toilet doors. One in every 11 commercials has a *direct* message about beauty, while countless others carry *indirect* messages about what makes girls and women beautiful. An overwhelming number of times each day, we are told what we should look like.

And the definition of beauty presented to us has become very narrow. It is now one colour, one shape, one size. The standards are impossible to obtain.

For a long time I have really hated the way I look. Some mornings before school when I look in

*the mirror I feel like crying as I am so ashamed
of the fact I have so many freckles. My mum
tells me they are cute but I know they mustn't
be as I never see anyone else in magazines or on
TV with freckles. Lindsay Lohan had them when
she was small but they are gone now. I wonder
how she did that? I would do anything to get rid
of mine.*

Maddie, 14

*I know the size that appears on the labels on my
clothes is just a number but it feels like a score.
And my size says 14. And that's an F for Fail.*

Juane, 16

The only reason we no longer see those gorgeous freckles Lindsay Lohan had in her first film, *The Parent Trap*, is that the actress and the people who have airbrushed her photos have gone to a lot of effort and expense to get rid of them. And the idea that size 14 is not good enough is a myth – actually, the average Australian woman is a size 16!

Slaves to fashion?

Most fashion models have an ultra-thin waif-like look. But did you know that during the last three decades, fashion and advertising models have grown steadily thinner, yet the average weight of women under 30 years of age has actually risen?

Australia's Next Top Model (ANTM) provides an insight into what goes on behind the scenes in the modelling world and the fashion industry. and it seems we are very curious. *ANTM* rates well. Really well. In fact, the premiere of series 5 entered the record books and became the most watched show on pay TV. Many of the viewers are teen girls and many of the contestants are teen girls. In 2010, of the 16 contestants, only two are out of their teens and the average age was just 17.

What type of messages about beauty does the *Next Top Model* brand pass on to us?

I will never forget an episode of the American version of the show in which the contestants had to pose as victims of violent crimes for a fashion shoot. They were depicted shot, bashed, pushed down stairs. The images were graphic and deeply disturbing. But apparently, violence against women is so hot right now. The judges made remarks like: 'What's great about this is that you can also look beautiful in death' and 'Death becomes you, young lady.'

Even more disturbingly, the 'victims' were all meant to have been killed by other models. It was so over the top that it would have been laughable if it wasn't so creepy: 'Diana poses – organs stolen by a model.' What was the other model meant to have done with the stolen kidneys? Sold them for a Prada handbag?

The modelling industry is infamous for cattiness and the Australian series has seen some awful bullying. A few years back, the judges reprimanded contestants who had bullied Alamela Rowan, though they stopped short of punishing them. The main bully, Demelza Reveley, ended up winning the series and going on to receive lucrative modelling contracts – there, that showed her, didn't it?

The judges have sometimes been less-than-ideal role models, many of them doling out harsh criticism and calling contestants things like 'wild pig'.

In 2009 there was a revolution of sorts at *ANTM*, when a 'plus-sized model', Tahnee Atkinson, won. She was a size 10. I say this was a 'revolution of sorts' as the average Australian woman is a size 16. It was hardly an earth-shattering move, was it? And even then, 'in the fickle and unfair world of modelling it probably won't equal a long-term fashion career. As casting agents politely explained in the show, she just doesn't have the matchstick-thin figure required by most top designers,' wrote Georgia Waters of the *Brisbane Times*.

There has been so much general concern over poor body image among young people that the minister for youth in 2009, Kate Ellis, put together a Body Image Advisory group, which was chaired by Mia Freedman, who used to be the editor of *Cosmopolitan*. It featured big names in 'mandatory' = compulsory; required

the fashion industry and media, such as the producer and host of *ANTM*, Sarah Murdoch, children's health and psychology experts and leaders of youth organisations.

The group set a Body Image Code of Conduct and asked the fashion industry to adopt it. One of the things they asked was for designers to offer a greater diversity of sizes. The next season, *ANTM* chose not to adopt that recommendation. In fact, one 16-year-old contestant wasn't allowed on the catwalk because she was 'too big'. She was a size 8. She says the experience left her feeling embarrassed and shamed into changing her eating habits. How crazy is that?

Mia Freedman became so fed up with the lack of change that she came out and publicly admitted that the advisory group got it wrong by not making the code mandatory so that the fashion industry would be forced to follow it. She wrote: 'Apart from a few notable exceptions (*Shop Til You Drop* consistently feature a diverse mix of "real women" of all shapes, sizes and nationalities on their shopping pages as well as a plus-sized monthly columnist) NOTHING HAS CHANGED. The Body Image Code of Conduct has been given the fashionable middle finger by those it was aimed at.'

Good on her for speaking out. I wish the government would not only join her in saying they got it wrong, too, but would start to act, because you know what? The definition of beauty hasn't always been this narrow.

'voluptuous' = sensual and curvy

Various shapes and sizes have been considered ideal throughout history. In the seventeenth century, the time that Rubens was painting his masterpieces, fuller-figured women were highly desirable as their curves were an indication of wealth. Only poor working women were thin, so thinness was associated with being lower class. In the 1950s, the voluptuous actress Marilyn Monroe was considered the ultimate sex goddess (although even she was not happy and lived with constant self-doubt). She dated presidents, sports stars and gangsters, was adored and imitated but today would probably be told by movie executives to lose weight.

Diet crazy

Fast forward and what do Hollywood celebrities look like now? I found a T-shirt online with a saying that I think sums it up perfectly. It was by designer Patricia Field and it was called the Trash and Luxury Celebrity Diet shirt: 'Another amazing celeb inspired tee. The celebrity diet, and our diet. Complete with a balanced cigarette, and some pills . . . any pills.' No doubt it was meant as a joke – but it actually does represent the current celebrity stick-thin female ideal, don't you think?

Hollywood stars are literally banking on their looks, but they aren't the only ones who are obsessed with the body beautiful. Many of us have dieting down to an art form, too, substituting cigarettes, pills and weird diet supplements for real food. Some purge through vomiting or using laxatives, or have surgery.

Our relationship with food, which surely should be so simple, seems to have become incredibly complex. Health experts warn that we are in the midst of an obesity epidemic. Up to 54 per cent of the adult population may be overweight. Meanwhile, large numbers of us routinely go on diets: as many as 50 per cent of teenage girls say they have been on a diet.

Did you know that tragically, all this dieting and suffering does not even work? Within two years, 95 per cent of people who go on weight-loss diets, including commercial diets, regain all the weight they lost, plus more. No wonder the weight-loss industry is worth billions of dollars each year: once its slave, we are forever in its service.

Then there is the even darker side of weight loss: the eating disorders anorexia and bulimia. Many of us have self-doubt and days when we wish we were more attractive. For some, however, mental illness and a serious body–mind disconnect may arise. Although people of all ages and both sexes are affected by eating disorders, they are most common in adolescent girls and young women.

It is estimated that between 2 and 5 per cent of

teenage girls could be anorexic or bulimic. However, the true number is probably much higher because many cases of eating disorders, particularly bulimia, go undetected. Some recent studies have shown the real rate may be as high as 20 per cent – that's one in five – among students. At least one in five teen girls resort to extreme dieting measures, such as laxatives.

A Victorian study of kids aged 12 to 17 years showed 38 per cent of girls and 12 per cent of boys were intermediate to extreme dieters – that is, they were at risk of an eating disorder. A Sydney study of children aged 11 to 15 reported that 16 per cent of the girls and 7 per cent of the boys had already used at least one potentially dangerous method of weight reduction, including starvation, vomiting and laxative abuse.

It has become accepted that we should all be dissatisfied with our bodies and should all be striving to become thinner, more toned, a more 'perfect' shape. As Courtney Martin says in her book *Perfect Girls, Starving Daughters*, 'We can be well educated, creative, capable, experienced, and still not have the capacity to figure out how to free ourselves from guilt over every little thing we put in our mouths.'

The new normality of hating one's body is evident everywhere. It certainly rates well on TV. The advertisements for the Australian version of the ultimate diet show, *The Biggest Loser*, have featured sad, lonely-looking people – depicted in shades of grey – who want far more than just a healthy body, it seems to me. 'I just want to be like every other girl,' one contestant, Nicola, declared. Nicola did lose weight, dramatically. Yes, after much blood, sweat, tears and a good dose of public humiliation, she got her 'reveal', a night when all the contestants paraded their new bodies to gasping audiences. I don't know whether she got the acceptance and love she so obviously craved, but the irony was that Nicola already was like every other girl: she saw her body as the enemy.

That year, *The Biggest Loser*'s theme song was Beck's 'Everyone's Gotta Learn Sometimes', which includes the lyrics 'I need your lovin.' Isn't that what we all really crave – love? It's just that some of us get lost and think we may find love in food and then get bewildered when society tells us we will find it only through our hunger. There is a known link between our emotions and what we eat, yet it seems to be largely ignored by all the hype that surrounds each diet fad or regime that seductively promises a new life through a new body.

Becoming skinny doesn't guarantee us happiness or love.

> There is a huge amount of pressure on girls to be thin.
>
> Anon., 15

*The hardest thing about being a teenage girl is
living with the media telling us continuously how
to look.*

Anon., 15

Body battle on the sports field

It seems obvious that we should all try to get regular exercise to stay fit and healthy, but so often advertising and the media focus on a less healthy motivation. Being a woman itself is portrayed as a competitive sport. Exercising is not so much about being fit as about trying to perfect our appearance. This, we are told, will make us more desirable, give us an advantage over other women and make them envious.

Skins, a range of sportswear for women, offered some ultra-destructive messages in one of their campaigns: 'Men will love you, women will hate you. Lucky you're not a lesbian. Skins delivers immediate results for the woman who wants to look and feel like a complete bitch.' Or how about: 'Get a body to die for. And watch women queue up to help with your funeral arrangements. Skins are perfect for the woman who loves the feel of claws sticking into her back.'

The emphasis on playing sport or exercising just as a means of obtaining the perfect body is ugly enough, but pitting woman against woman? Gross.

Also ugly was the Brooks Sports ad that promoted the company's support of breast cancer treatment. This is a great cause, but their promotion featured two female runners with their breasts bouncing and the caption 'Nice pair!'

Sportswomen already don't get the recognition they deserve. Did you know that horse racing receives more TV airtime in Australia than all women's sport combined? The last thing women need is for advertisers to trivialise us as just a pair of tits in sneakers!

Because the message of these ads is to exercise just to look hot, hot, hot, they feed the very real risk of girls overexercising as a means of controlling weight. Research clearly shows that overexercising and eating disorders go hand in hand.

These ads also alienate girls and women who may not be comfortable with ruthless competition, nor with being viewed as sex objects while exercising. It is not always easy to get motivated to exercise and messages such as these really don't help.

When the Australian Senate had an inquiry into female participation in sport, it concluded that female sportswear might be stopping some girls and women from exercising. They called for sportswear that is flattering, comfortable and practical.

If your sports uniforms are a cause of body anxiety for you, try speaking to your school to see if you can have some input into designing them. Perhaps options could be provided to allow more personal choice, such as looser designs. (I know you might be thinking that your school won't listen, but if you put together a strong proposal and deliver it respectfully, they should at least hear you out – true?)

Girls and women urgently need more positive messages about being fit and healthy and participating in sport, such as this Adidas women's campaign: 'Play a sport where the rewards are respect, self-belief and inner strength. Play by your own rules. Play gym. Impossible is nothing.' Yes!

The camera always lies

So much of the idea of beauty that we are trying to live up to is not even real. The trend towards digitally manipulating away supposed imperfections – including those features that make us unique and interesting – affects virtually every image we see in advertisements and many of the images we see of celebrities. Once the photographer's job was to capture what was beautiful and individual about a model or star. Today, their photographs are altered until they fit a socially accepted standard of flawless beauty.

But it is not just the glossy magazines and advertisers that crop, colour, erase and enhance their images.

Ordinary people want a bit of the action, too. There is a roaring trade in touching up photos for Facebook and other social networking sites, and in airbrushing school photos. Cheekbones are elongated; freckles are banished; braces are even removed. A Melbourne school made news when some of the female students found their school photos had been altered without their permission. How would you feel if your school photos came back and your hairstyle had been adjusted or your earrings covered over?

I know I have plenty of school photos of me in which I look awkward, yet I love them as they offer an insight into what I was like as a growing girl. In fact, I always start my work with girls in schools by sharing with them my Year 4 class photo. We all laugh at my tragic cut-with-a-bowl-on-top-of-my-head haircut and the skivvy I was wearing under my uniform to hide my arm. The photo was not perfect, but it was me!

How much longer until all the images we see of women will blur into the one uniform, unobtainable version of beauty?

We play the 'compare and despair' game, comparing images of women who seem perfect, but are not real, to our bodies, which are real. And for some, despair turns to a desire to cut and paste – not on a computer screen, but in real life.

Plastic not so fantastic

Our differences, our imperfections and our physical scars make us unique. Yet the messages we receive through the media tell us that our differences set us apart for all the wrong reasons.

Celebrities are beginning to morph into one another. Many feature the same bee-stung lips, chiselled cheekbones, wide eyes and wrinkle-free brow. Just think of Madonna, Demi Moore, Liz Hurley. Women are no longer permitted to age and must remain forever taut and trim. Cosmetic surgery is being sold to women as just being 'refreshed' and 'rejuvenated'. And can it really be so bad when it seems that just about everyone is doing it?

Yes, it really can be. Take Heidi Montag, who was an ordinary teenager when she appeared in *The Hills*. She became famous simply as a result of being famous. And in her quest for even more fame, she had at least ten cosmetic procedures . . . *in one day*. That was in addition to a number of other times she had already gone under the knife. She had a chin reduction, a brow lift, buttock augmentation, her ears pinned back, two nose jobs, two breast enhancements and more. By 24, she was broke and wishing she never had the surgeries.

'Sometimes I wish I could go back to the original Heidi,' she said. For Heidi, fame brought with it enormous insecurity — and she believed that surgery could fix that. Once she was on TV, she had to hear strangers 'rejuvenation' = the process of being made youthful again

talking about her 'horse face' and big chin. When she appeared in *Playboy*, the magazine said her breasts were too small, and then digitally enhanced them.

After two boob jobs, she got the breasts that *Playboy* wanted – but she was miserable. 'If I could take it back, I would,' she said. When she was asked for her advice to other young women planning to have cosmetic surgery, she said, 'I would tell them not to do it. You risk your life when you go under the knife every time, so is that worth your life?'

Unfortunately, plenty of women do still seem to think it's worth it. I was asked to go on television and discuss the self-confessed British plastic surgery addict Sarah Burge, who gave her seven-year-old daughter a voucher for a breast enlargement for her birthday. Crazy much?

While it is easy to dismiss these women as wannabes, the fact remains that plastic surgery and other cosmetic procedures are being used by women in the mainstream as a means of seeking the attention and validation they crave. And it seems that it is no longer enough to have a facelift or a boob job, or to have some collagen injected in the lips. Vaginal 'rejuvenation' procedures are now popular, too. It seems everything female needs to be reshaped.

It is not that hard to understand why women might want faces and bodies that look more like the stars', but why the desire for a designer vagina? Researcher Karen Roberts McNamara notes that 'in years past, women rarely had the opportunity to see other women's vaginas and thus had no sense of how a typical vagina might look. Yet with the mainstreaming of the adult entertainment industry, the situation has changed dramatically. Now, a beauty standard has emerged, one established primarily through porn actresses, nude models and strippers.'

She argues that women are going under the scalpel to have their vaginal openings tightened and their labias made smaller because they have been convinced this will 'normalise' them and give them confidence. The plastic surgery industry's 'sanitized ideal of the clean, delicate, discreet vaginal slit' casts the bodies of women who have not undergone these procedures 'as necessarily dirty and unsightly'.

Speaking of overly groomed vaginas (now there's a phrase I bet you weren't expecting to read when you started this book!) reminds me of one of the most astounding moments in talk-show history. It was when Jennifer Love Hewitt discussed on American TV that she had devoted an entire chapter of her book on relationships to decorating her hairless pubic mound with jewelled decals – a practice known as 'vajazzling' that is gaining in popularity here, too.

Hewitt told her host, 'Women should vajazzle their vajayjays . . . It really helped me.' She went on to say, 'After a break-up, a friend of mine Swarovski-crystalled my precious lady . . . and it shined like a disco ball.' It really 'empowered' her, she insisted (although apparently she was not quite empowered enough to use adult terms for her anatomy).

Forget the war on terrorism – if the amount of ads for decorating, shaving, waxing and electrolysis are anything to go by, it is the age of the war on women's vaginas.

Of course it's not just grown women who are being told they should doubt their own genitals. During recent formal seasons, beauticians have noted a huge increase in the number of young women wanting 'intimate' grooming treatments. Girls as young as 14 are asking for Brazilian waxes. A school in New Zealand for students from Year 1 to 13 ran a beauty salon's ad for Brazilian waxing in the school diary. Imagine pulling out your five-year-old sister's homework diary and an ad for Brazilian waxing jumping out at you!

With all the pressure to wax and vajazzle and 'rejuvenate', we seem to have lost sight of what 'normal' is. In an episode of the UK's *The Sex Education Show*, when teens of both sexes were shown images of women with pubic hair, they gasped in what seemed to be shock or disgust. The producers had set out to show that in reality 'we all come in all different shapes and sizes. From penises to pubes, bums to boobs whatever you've got it's all perfectly normal.'

I am taking up this call-to-arms by blogger Amanda Hess :

> For now, the more extreme performances of femininity, like breast implantation, vaginal 'rejuvenation,' and Vajazzling aren't considered the norm for women. I'm not going to be met with shock when I remove my pants and reveal to my sex partner that I haven't converted my pubic mound into a shiny disco ball. But these days, it wouldn't be out of the ordinary for him to be shocked that I'm not perfectly waxed. The body hair ship may have sailed, but vaginal modification is at a point right now where we are still in a position to fend off the tide. And my greatest fear is that someday, we will wake to find that our girls are being routinely Vajazzled upon puberty, and realize that we never stood up to say, 'This . . . is . . . *ridiculous.*'

It is important to realise we have the power to resist and change the harmful stereotypes presented to girls and women as the ideals for which we must strive.

We have the power to create our own new body-loving reality.

We have an obligation – to ourselves and to our friends – to end the madness.

You with me?

Action plan

Focus on more than just your looks. When I tell my daughters they are beautiful, I make sure I praise at least two other qualities in them that I also admire, e.g. 'You are beautiful *and* smart, funny, kind-hearted, passionate, strong, brave, intelligent . . .'

Tell yourself this message, too. When you look at a picture of yourself, don't assess its Facebook worthiness based only on how hot you look in it. Ask yourself: 'Do I look happy?' or 'Was that a day I really showed how strong I can be?'

Australia's sex discrimination commissioner and the commissioner responsible for age discrimination, Elizabeth Broderick, told me she has long chats about body image with her daughter, who she believes is far more concerned with body image than she was as a girl. Elizabeth told me, 'I asked her once "Who loves Lucy the best?" She answered, "Mummy, Daddy." I corrected her: "No, Lucy must love Lucy the best."'

When I was at school, the ultimate girl-crime was to love yourself. The insults would fly: 'You so love yourself!' 'She thinks she's all that.' 'She is so up herself.' Isn't that bizarre? Seems we are threatened by a girl with inner-Amazon powers.

Break the mould. You don't need to think you are better than the other girls around you, rather that you are unique and have worth.

Tell your friends you love them because they are beautiful *and for reasons other than just their looks, too.* During our Enlighten workshops, girls write their friends positive affirmations. I cannot begin to tell you how much these notes mean to the girls who receive them. There is always at least one girl who is so happy that she cries! Don't you just love happy tears? I get emails like this one from Lillie all the time and they rock my soul:

I loved you, you seriously changed my life forever i will remember you, ! you probably don't remember me as you have meet probably a million girls, and the day i saw you i cried, but i didn't want to because i thought the other girls would laugh at me but when we got on the bus to go back to school all the girls were telling me how pretty i was and how everyone loves me and a lot of other really nice comments, and it made me feel a million dollars. and now i am myself for ever and always not afraid of what people think, and if they like who i am, well i know they are liking the real me !!! thank you, l love Lillie. So thank you ! And when i got home i told my mum and yet i cried again and now i feel i can really tell my mum everything. xxxx

Lillie, 14 years

Choose your words carefully when you talk about your appearance and the way other girls look, too. Don't put yourself down just to get validation. I want to scream when I go on Facebook and see a girl upload a really beautiful picture of herself that you just know she loves, and she writes a description like: 'Not sure if I like this shot, what do you guys think?' She is obviously desperate for external validation. Would it be so bad to just upload the pic and then add a smiley face perhaps? Or 'Am happy with this!'

I will admit most of my Facebook profile pictures are fairly glam (in my mind anyway!) as I am fortunate to have had a number of professional photo shoots done through my work in the media. Just to show I do not need to define myself by these glossy snapshots, I once uploaded a picture my son took of me having my teeth checked at the dentist. I look gruesome in this image – hello, does anyone look hot with their mouth wide open and dental instruments hanging out? I loved the fact that many of my friends then uploaded images of themselves looking real, too – after they'd applied a face mask, or with morning hair. It was really liberating! I started a Facebook page where girls and women could upload their kick-arse Amazon-confidence pictures. It's called 'Lovin' me – whether I'm looking feral or fab!'

Whether we are looking rocking or shocking, let's agree that the ultimate girl-crime should not be to love ourselves! Accept compliments graciously and give them generously. And don't forget, all girls and women can be hypersensitive about references to their bodies and are excellent at picking up even subtle messages. Any snide remarks you make about another person's weight or appearance will be absorbed into the soul. No one wants to be a soul scarrer.

Engage in healthy diet and exercise rather than pushing yourself to lose weight. One of the most practical ways to boost your body image is to become involved in sports. Research both here and in the United States has found that women who participate in sports and physical activity have a more positive body image than those who don't. Participation in sports brings approval from peers, family and friends, and helps women feel that they are capable and competent. These positive feelings produce a positive body image.

Find a sport you enjoy. I was never a team player as I was not very physically coordinated (in other words, I was unco). But I discovered I love doing weights and running. Pop me on a treadmill with some cool tunes (hello, Paul Dempsey) and I can go at my own pace and I am happy. Find what feeds your body and soul.

Watch for early warning signs of a serious body-image crisis in yourself and your friends. Signs of an eating disorder may include any or a combination of the following:

dramatic weight loss, constant dieting, excessive exercising, social withdrawal, a fixation with food, a change in appetite (either refusing to eat or bingeing) and insomnia.

Some girls self-harm, cutting their bodies, especially arms or upper legs. Girls who self-harm may also burn or hit themselves. Warning signs include scars or frequent unexplained injuries. This is often a response to stress and anxiety about body image, academic expectations or destructive relationships.

If any of the above sounds like you, or you have a friend who is showing any of these warning signs, it should be brought to the attention of an adult you trust.

Navigate the media. Although I do not think the media are solely responsible for the objectification of women, I do think they play a key role. Pay attention to what you read, watch and listen to. Be a critical viewer of popular culture. Deconstruct media messages. Be an active viewer and reader, rather than passively absorbing media.

Ask yourself, 'Why are all the actresses on this show the same body shape and size?', 'How do I feel about my body after reading that magazine?' or 'Will it be easy for this contestant to maintain that body shape after they leave the program?'

Start a Detox Diary. Despite what the media tell us, our bodies are not toxic. We do not constantly need to detox to purge and rid ourselves of poisons. Yet our minds may be in need of a cleanse. A Detox Diary is a record of healing and of your journey from hating to

'cathartic' = bringing a feeling of renewal or release, through purging or cleansing

loving your own body. The following are just some of the things that can be included:

+ images of women who inspire you
+ notes and letters from friends that make you feel good about yourself
+ affirmations such as 'I am happy with the way I look' or 'I accept my body the way it is'
+ quotes that motivate you
+ photographs of you looking and feeling happy.

Your diary should not focus on negative thoughts, fears and insecurities about your body. While writing such things down can be cathartic, I believe there is also a real risk that it encourages you to obsess on the negatives, revisiting them over and over and reopening old wounds. It is kind of like vomiting into a bag and keeping that vomit forever so that you can occasionally reopen it and have another sniff. Let. It. Go!

Appreciate your body. Women's bodies are amazing. I could not believe it when I first breastfed: how did my breasts know how to create milk? My body instinctively held the secret to nourishing life. Instead of critiquing yourself, celebrate the parts of your body you are pleased with. Focus on the positive aspects and give them a new emphasis.

See yourself as a whole person. You are more than just your breasts, your butt, your thighs – just as I am so much more than my arm. When we see ourselves and other girls and women – including our friends, mothers and teachers – as just bodies, we forget that we are all actually *somebodies*.

I was once shocked by a conversation I had with a teacher after I had just spent an amazing day with her students, who had been captivated and loved every minute of it. This teacher had sat talking (loudly) to other members of staff the whole time. I thought she had not listened to a word.

I was only partially correct. That evening, as I was about to address the girls' parents, she said to me, 'I heard parts of your opening talk to the girls this morning. You were burnt? Doesn't matter. At least your face is still pretty.' What could I say to this? She had missed the point entirely: my real beauty has very little to do with any physical part of me.

Fortunately, it seemed her students had heard my message. Each of these girls had lined up to kiss and hug me at the end of the day. When they told me I was beautiful, I knew they had seen all of me.

See all of yourself and all of the women in your life.

Seek out healthy role models. In a world where trashy celebrities adorn most magazines, it can be challenging to find good female role models, but it is an important quest. Find girls and women who seem to be at peace with their bodies and watch, listen and learn. I am a huge believer that you become like the people you hang around – insecurity rubs off, yet so does confidence. I love it when teens I work with tell me about some of the celebrity role models they have sought out:

> Jessica Mauboy; she's just so chill, with a BIG self-esteem; she's so beautiful and has an amazing voice.
>
> Stephanie, 16

> Pink – she is a great singer and she doesn't care what other people think – she is just herself no matter what people say.
>
> Emma, 13 (well, I'm turning 13 lol)

> Kate Winslet – she is stunning and intelligent, and most importantly, she has spoken out against being Photoshopped in magazine shoots.
>
> Claudia, 17

My daughter Teyah and I have both been drawn to a fictional female role model, Wonder Woman. And we do not love her just for her star-spangled ensemble. Wonder

Woman is one very smart sister. When all the other super-heroes lined up for their superpowers, they asked for things such as X-ray vision, the ability to sling webs or superhuman speed. Wonder Woman, an Amazon, asked for the 'lasso of truth'. Her gold rope surrounds the bad guys and forces them to speak words of truth to her. Words do have such power, the words we are surrounded by and those we use ourselves.

Claudia made a great point: actress Kate Winslet is one of the few Hollywood stars who tells it like it is. She once said in an interview:

> I don't want the next generation, your daughters and mine, growing up thinking that you have to be thin to look beautiful in certain clothes. It's terrifying right now. It's out of control. It's beyond out of control . . . I feel an enormous responsibility to stay normal and true to myself and not conform and all those things. You know? To be healthy. And normal. And to like to eat cake.

May the truth set us free from the myth of the ideal woman. We all deserve to eat cake.

Affirmations

I am more than my body; I am my heart, soul and mind.
My body is strong, unique and beautiful.

2

Beyond Generation Bratz

Most dolls for little girls represent teenage girls or women. One exception is Mattel's My Scene, Growing Up Glam doll, which depicts a tween, a girl somewhere between eight and 12 years old. She is dressed in lacy stockings, short skirt, diamanté belt and midriff top. Her accessories? A teddy bear and schoolbooks.

Twist the screw on her back – oh, how symbolic! – and her abdomen stretches. It's gruesome to watch. She looks as though she is being stretched by a medieval torture device. And hey presto, now she's a 'curvy, cool teen'. But wait, you say, all that has really changed is that her stomach has stretched to make her appear taller.

It seems that in Mattel land there is no difference

between an eight-year-old girl and an 18-year-old one. Nor should the clothes they wear differ. The only things that change once she has stretched before our very eyes into a 'curvy, cool teen' are her accessories. She trades in her schoolbooks and teddy bear for a full make-up kit, complete with false eyelashes – 'Whoa, her make-up changes!' – and some glossy fashion magazines. Flat shoes are out; it's all about stilettos now. Out, too, with cute hair clips and in with designer sunnies.

Where do I begin in explaining why I think this type of doll is so toxic?

'Curvy.' This is not a word that used to be associated with little girls or even with girls in their early teens. Yet look around. We now live in a culture that tells girls that being hot and sexy – and useless – is *way* cool.

Teen girls like you are increasingly being portrayed in a highly sexualised way and even your younger sisters are being encouraged to be sexy. Are we really all okay with that?

Too sexy, too soon

Many people – including leading experts in education, health and psychology – have serious concerns that our culture imposes pressure on girls to be too sexy, too soon.

We aren't talking about the healthy development

of sexuality here. It is perfectly normal to explore your sexuality as you grow and develop; and there is nothing wrong with receiving age-appropriate information and education about sex.

'cognitive' = involving thinking, reasoning or remembering

What *is* wrong is when a child has sexuality imposed on them. This is known by experts as 'sexualisation'. The American Psychological Association (APA) defines 'sexualisation' as when:

+ a person's value comes only from their sexual appeal;
+ their sexiness is judged according to a narrow ideal of physical attractiveness; or
+ they are sexually objectified – that is, seen simply as an object for others' sexual use.

These elements can all be seen, to varying degrees, in girls' toys, videos and magazines. There is a lot of research showing that exposure to sexualised imagery is linked to children experiencing increased anxiety, depression, low self-esteem, body-image problems, eating disorders and self-harm. The APA reported that sexualisation has a negative effect on girls' 'cognitive functioning, physical and mental health, sexuality and beliefs'. The Australian Psychological Society is so concerned that it has released guidelines for parents regarding the early sexualisation of children. The good news is, there is plenty we can all do together to put an end to this!

~∞~

In the toy store

The vile Growing Up Glam tween-to-teen doll is certainly not alone in promoting a sexy look. Good old Barbie – sometimes a teacher, astronaut or even a US presidential candidate – is doused in glitter, wears micro-miniskirts and has all the party-girl accessories. Mattel's Bling Bling Bikini doll comes with bikini, stilettos, thick make-up, optional bling bling spa and what looks to me like a pina colada cocktail as an accessory.

Sportz Bratz declares: 'It is not how you play the game, it's how hot you look when you win.' Even baby dolls have been given the sexed-up treatment. The Bratz Babyz range featured toddlers wearing G-string-style nappies, fish-nets, leather micro-minis and chain belts. These baby dolls went way beyond prams: they came complete with Harley-Davidson motorbikes.

Does it really matter? Yes. It really does. Childhood plus the adult world of fish-nets, booze, and grown-up confidence and attitude makes a dangerous combination. Agree?

It would be too simplistic to argue that dolls alone are responsible for girls not feeling pretty or thin or popular enough. And you know what, I loved Barbie as a young girl and I think I turned out just fine. So I am not trying to be the Toy Police here or judge you if you and your friends enjoyed playing with these toys, or your younger sisters are playing with them now. What I do want to do is encourage you to think critically about the messages these toys send. Fair enough?

And I want to pose a couple of questions for you to think about: Girls mature physically and emotionally more rapidly than boys and also tend to be more quickly immersed in popular culture, so your childhood is already particularly brief. So why are the adults who market these toys eroding your younger sisters' little-girl time even more rapidly? Why are there so many cultural pressures on *you* to grow up too fast also, and to believe that your girl power lies in your ability to be *way* sexy?

And if it is okay to buy a lingerie-clad Bratz Baby reclining on a revolving bed under a disco light, just what is off limits for girls?

At the magazine stand

The fact is that currently nothing seems to be off limits. Even media that say they care about and empower girls have sold them out by sexing them up. *Girlpower* is an Australian magazine aimed at girls aged from 7 to 12. When I was flipping through an issue with Teyah a few years back, I found images that were anything but empowering. They included a poster of Ashlee Simpson for little girls to put on their bedroom walls. It showed the singing star wearing a man's suit with no top underneath and not even a bra. She was pulling the waistband of her trousers down to show more of her crotch and though she didn't show her nipple, her left breast was mostly exposed. Ashlee's real source of power – her voice – was negated: her mouth was shut. Her eyes were downcast and much of her face was veiled by her long blonde hair. It was all about her body.

The same issue also included a 'Hotness Scale' that encouraged small girls to have a crush on Nick Lachey. Then aged 35, the singer and former husband of pop diva Jessica Simpson was older than many of their fathers. Also singled out was 23-year-old Chace Crawford, a star of *Gossip Girl*. That's an M-rated TV show and therefore one they shouldn't even be watching yet.

Would you want your eight-year-old little sister watching that show? Surely Jessica Simpson's ex and an actor who plays a bad-boy pothead who needs to go to rehab are not ideal boyfriends for little girls.

Magazines that encourage primary-school-age girls to have crushes on men are playing a dangerous game with their minds. Parents do their best to protect their children. To cultivate mature men as romantic ideals for little girls seems at odds with those efforts.

It is actually impossible for parents to critique many of the magazines aimed at primary-school-aged girls before purchasing them, as they are sealed in plastic to protect all the giveaways they entice readers with.

Yet men's magazines, also displayed at children's eye height in supermarkets, are not sealed in plastic and can be looked at by anyone, no matter how young. Magazines such as *FMH*, *Ralph* and *Zoo*, showing scantily clad bikini babes on the front, are purchased at all our major supermarkets while grabbing the milk and bread. I don't want my little boy viewing soft porn while I am grabbing cordial off the shelf. Do you ever feel uncomfortable when this type of magazine is right in your face at the shops?

Elements of the soft-porn men's magazine world meet the teen-girl world head-on by the time you get into magazines such as *Girlfriend* and *Dolly*. And why wouldn't parents buy these mags for their daughters? *Girlfriend* calls itself 'a girl's best friend' and says it focuses on empowering girls. Yet it ran a giveaway of Playboy T-shirts. Readers were told:

> Playboy is a collection of clothing and swimwear for
> the trend savvy fashionable girl. Cute and innocent,
> cool and tough, all at the same time. Playboy is one
> brand you should include in your wardrobe.

I worked with Year 5 girls at a school and around a quarter of them claimed they read *Girlfriend*. One girl also proudly told me that she already had a Playboy T-shirt, too. 'It's really cute,' she said. 'It is striped with the bunny on the left corner.' (The teachers later told me that this little girl's naivety paled in comparison to that of another girl who, at a school camp, wore a T-shirt with the slogan 'Wrap your lips around this' emblazoned across the front. The girl, who happened to be a particularly reserved child, had no idea how inappropriate this was. Apparently, nor did her parents.)

Playboy has long been a leading brand in the pornography industry, but now it is becoming part of the mainstream. This is because Playboy's profits were falling, so they started selling the rights to put the bunny logo on all sorts of products, such as pencil cases, doona covers and movies. The Easter bunny even visited the Playboy mansion in the family film *Hop*. And a Playboy jewellery line was launched at Diva, where lots of little girls and teens shop.

It seems the media and marketers want us to view this brand, which makes money out of girls getting naked to please men, as nothing more than harmless, mainstream fun. Is it just me or is Hugh Hefner-as-a-cool-dude a world of wrong? Hello peeps, he is an 80+-year-old man living with a group of 20-year-old women who share his bed at the Mansion. Wrong much? (*Danni does a little vomit in her mouth.*)

Before you buy one of these products, all I ask is that

you think about what the bunny represents and what wearing it truly means. Is it a fashion statement or a walking advertisement for a porn company?

I think it was hypocritical for a teen magazine such as *Girlfriend* to claim to empower girls while promoting a brand related to the porn industry. Not to mention that the publishers who produce *Girlfriend* also once published *Explode*, a magazine for teen boys that boasted 'all the eye candy you can handle'. Sounds like blatant objectification of girls' bodies to me. Would you like to be referred to as mere eye candy?

Have you ever noticed how many of the ads at the back of *Girlfriend* and *Dolly* are for highly sexual ringtones and wallpaper downloads? Do they offer a healthy perspective on girls and sexuality? 'Save a virgin, do me instead.' 'Fancy a quickie anyone?' 'Sex – when it's good, it's really good, when it's bad, it's still pretty good.'

Some of the information on sex in these magazines is very informative and sensible. I have to admit that in recent years when my daughter has bought *Dolly* I have found some of the issues really great. I even rang the editor, Tiffany Dunk, to tell her this (hey, credit where credit is due). *Girlfriend* interviewed me for an article they were doing on teen friendships and again, the story was really spot on.

I want to be fair here: I appreciate that magazines can and do play an important role in educating girls about sexuality. Yet I fear that in some cases they risk leading their readers to think that if they are not yet sexually active, they are missing out.

In the results of a sex survey in *Dolly*, 21 per cent of readers were quoted as claiming to have lost their virginity at between 10 and 13 years of age. The legal age of consent is 16. There are good reasons for this: research shows that girls who become sexually active at a young age are at a much higher lifelong risk of sexually transmitted diseases and that even once a girl is physically mature, it takes years for her to be psychologically and emotionally ready for sex. The *Dolly* results show that either a lot of young girls are at risk – or a lot of young girls exaggerate, as they think sexiness equates to coolness. Just over half of the readers said they had given oral sex to a boy.

There is a very real risk that magazine readers will think that to fit in they have to be sexually experienced. No one likes to feel left out.

If you listened to what the other girls talked about at school, you'd think everyone was having sex constantly! Like they are rabbits or something! I think most of them are making it up but it is still tough as you kind of feel like if no guy has tried to do anything with you yet, well maybe that's because you're ugly or something.

Joanne, 14

When I started dating my boyfriend in Year 8 all his mates said I had to give him head in front of them near the canteen at lunch. I was so scared. I pretended I was sick for a week before my mum finally got me to tell her what was happening. She was really shocked but really, most girls at my school had done this before and they told me I was just being straight and that he would break up with me if I didn't.

Lauren, 13

I guess what I am trying to say here is: read whichever magazines you'd like to (I trust you can make good choices) *but* be mindful. Keep your eyes and ears open. Question what you read. And if you see things that don't feel right, let the editors know. Amazon girls are never silent!

On the internet

For many of you, pornography will be your first experience with sex. Porn is nothing new but it has never been more accessible than it is today, thanks to the internet and mobile phones. In the 2009 UK television series *The Sex Education Show*, three out of ten high school students interviewed said they learnt about sex predominantly through viewing pornography on the internet and mobiles or in magazines. When I talk to girls in schools, many tell me that they are expected to act and look like the images kids see on sex sites they view online. This helps explain the popularity of Brazilian waxes. Seeing the look modelled by the women on porn sites, it seems that exposing the genitals in this way will make a girl hotter.

The website girl.com.au claims to be empowering girls worldwide – but the word 'empowering' has become so misused in our society. I was on their home page a while back and it featured Play School, Fisher-Price, Barbie and Bratz, so their target audience would seem to have included very young girls. Yet by clicking through to another special page on girl.com.au, a reader would find a feature devoted to Brazilian waxing. Its advice for the little girls who logged on to be 'empowered' was:

> Brazilian waxing involves spreading hot wax on your
> buttocks and vagina area. A cloth is patted over the wax,
> then pulled off. Don't be alarmed if the waxer throws
> your legs over your shoulder, or asks you to moon them,
> this is normal and ensures there are no stray hairs. A
> tweezer is used for the more delicate areas (red bits).
> So why does it appeal? Nobody really likes hair in their
> private regions and it has a childlike appeal. Men love it,
> and are eternally curious about it.

Since when should vaginas have a 'childlike appeal'? After I exposed this incredibly dangerous advice on my blog, the company took out the line about children's genitals being appealing. However, the page on Brazilian waxing, along with features on such topics as how to be a 'witch in the bedroom', remained.

I have seen girls become so desensitised to X-rated images on the net that when boys send them pornographic pictures to their phones with messages like 'You should make your pussy look like this one', the girls simply laugh and forward the images on to other girls.

But I am betting that a lot of those girls laugh not because they think it is actually funny but to mask their embarrassment. Nervous laughter doesn't mean we're having fun, rather that we are feeling uncomfortable.

I really feel for you. You juggle schoolwork, complex teen-girl friendships and boys – all while feeling pressured to be beautiful and thin, cool and sophisticated. No wonder so many girls report feeling stressed, depressed and anxious.

I want to be very clear here: I am not advocating you lock yourself away in a tower. It is vital that you are informed about sex. And you know what? Sex between consenting partners is natural and can be enormous fun.

But to me it seems damaging for you to be influenced largely by porn images when you are just developing your own sexuality. The porn ideal of female sexuality is so narrow. Just as magazines and ads tell you that only a leggy size-8 model can be truly beautiful, the porn industry would have you believe that only a busty, wet and wild blonde can be truly sexy. It's all big (fake) breasts, pouts, pole dancing and male fantasies.

Women's (and men's) sexuality is, in reality, so much more diverse and complicated.

It may seem that the women you see in porn are all truly enjoying it and are somehow empowered by the experience of being in the sex industry. In fact, research shows that many only take part in it because they feel they have no other option. They may be financially desperate, drugged or even physically forced into it.

And often the porn you see on the net is not soft-core porn or even vanilla sex between consenting adults. Many sites show images that are explicit and sometimes kinky in ways that would disturb even a lot of adults. This is not liberation. This is not about girls feeling good and exploring their bodies and the bodies of their partners if they choose to. This is a very narrow Hugh-Heffneresque vision of sexuality. The images of sex online are largely devoid of relationship or meaning.

But it's not just images online that tell you being a woman is all about pole dancing and pubic hair maintenance . . .

In music videos

Song lyrics have always been filled with sexual innu-endo and pushed society's boundaries but the kind of in-your-face misogyny you hear in a lot of mainstream music is a relatively new thing. An extreme

'misogyny' = hatred of women

example would be Eminem, whose lyrics include this gem, from his song 'Kill You': '(AH!) Slut, you think I won't choke no whore, 'til the vocal cords don't work in her throat no more?!'

Researchers looked into whether listening to lyrics such as Eminem's increases sexist attitudes. They found little evidence that it did and therefore concluded there was little reason to suggest these songs be censored. But I don't think this research is enough to decide the question, because it didn't delve into the issue of girls' and women's body image. Even if sexist attitudes do not increase because of misogynistic music, how does it make girls and women feel about themselves and their bodies?

And how does it make boys view girls, and vice versa? The American Academy of Pediatrics has stated that exposure to misogynistic music that portrays violence against women and sexual coercion as normal may make it more difficult for teenagers to know what is normal in a relationship.

There also seems to be a recording industry rule that music videos have to sexually objectify women. Male stars seem unable to perform unless they're surrounded by numerous pert breasts and gyrating rears. Female stars apparently just can't sing if they're wearing more than

> 'demographic' = a group of people as defined by factors such as their age group, gender or social background

lingerie and maybe a belt. The camera angles used to film music videos are off-putting, too. More often than not, they seem to be shot with the camera looking up at the female performers' crotches. The girls I worked with at one school in New Zealand termed this technique 'crotch-cam'.

A British study found that watching video clips featuring skinny, semi-naked women – in other words, virtually all music clips – for just 10 minutes was enough to reduce teenage girls' satisfaction with their body shape by 10 per cent.

Yet this music is what adults now give children as the soundtrack to their youth. 'Hits for Kids, Pop Party 6' featured Hi 5, Justin Bieber and ... Lady Gaga's 'Bad Romance'. With lyrics such as 'I want your ugly, I want your disease ... I want your leather-studded kiss in the sand' it's great stuff for little kids, huh?

Lady Gaga is big with the tween demographic even though her songs and videos have always been ultra-sexy, dark and creepy. Even for me as an adult, watching the full version of 'Telephone' made me feel a bit sick. Lady Gaga gets thrown in a porn-fantasy version of a women's prison. There are violent assaults, sexual intimidation, graphic tongue kissing, smoking. Then Beyonce bails her out so they can go on a killing spree, murdering a mass of strangers by poisoning them.

'raunch culture' = the current sex-obsessed culture that encourages girls and women to feel that their worth depends on how hot they are

Along with Lady Gaga, 'Hits for Kids, Pop Party 6' also included 'Hush Hush'. That's by The Pussycat Dolls, five grown women who strut and pout their way through overtly sexy songs and had their origins in adult-only clubs. (Who can forget their timeless classic 'Don't cha wish your girlfriend was raw like me? Don't cha wish your girlfriend was fun like me?' Well, that one made it onto 'Hits for Kids, Volume 3.) Speaking of the Pussycat Dolls, they recently did some cross-promotional work with Supre in New Zealand and offered some 'lucky' teen shoppers the chance to have their photo taken back stage with the Dolls. Awesome (*sarcasm alert*).

Have you ever listened to song lyrics and thought they were just way too raunchy? Hello, I am looking at you, Ms 'Dirty Talk' Wynter Gordon.

Don't get me wrong, there have been amazing female singers and girl bands that have been all about power and strength – but today the groups most often said to be about girl power are really all about getting their gear off and pouting. The Pussycat Dolls, empowering? Lady Gaga in her underwear in a women's prison? I don't see girl power. What I see is raunch culture being sold as empowerment.

In clothes stores

How many times have you heard an adult say that girls dress too grown-up and act too raunchy? I am often asked by the media: 'Why do teen girls dress in such revealing clothes?' (*insert frown and look of disgust at teen-girls-gone-wild*) My response: girls are damned if they do and damned if they don't. On the one hand, the media and popular culture tell you to look hot and act sexy, on the other they make out that you are all 'sluts' or 'skanks' when you do.

Classic example: teen clothing brand Supré. Some of their ads seem wildly inappropriate. How about the jeggings campaign that showed a teen girl prancing around with just her jean/leggings on and only her hand strategically placed to cover her nipples? How about the T-shirts Supré have sold that have said such offensive things as 'Smoke to be thin', 'Santa's Pole Dancer' (a hit at Christmas, I'm sure) and 'Pussy Power'?

What gets me really mad is that people rarely question *the brand* that dishes this up, but rather *the girls* who buy into the marketing hype. You've probably heard of the Facebook pages 'Luring sluts into my bedroom with a trail of Supré vouchers' (more than 137,000 fans) and 'Kidnapping sluts from Supré and selling them in the used section on eBay'. I want to find the people who set these sites up and tell them what the real deal is: there is no reason to ever call another girl a slut or a skank. Full stop. And there is no excuse for someone to assume they know things about a girl's sexuality based just on how she dresses. You with me?

In her fabulous book for teen girls, *Your Skirt Is Too Short*, feminist Emily Maguire tells it how it is:

> Amongst the women I know there is absolutely no way you could guess who has slept with the most men simply by looking. Hell, look at me in my baggy jeans and overcoat and try and guess my sexual history . . .
>
> You see a woman in a dress that reveals a lot of skin: maybe her choice of clothing signifies a desire for attention. Maybe it signifies that she is part of mainstream fashion culture. Maybe she loves the colour or fabric. Maybe she wants to keep cool while out dancing. It's not the right of others to pass judgment on what a woman is 'saying' or 'asking for' by dressing in a particular way . . .
>
> Let's get real: teenage girls do sometimes wear skimpy clothes. You can sort of see how some older people might make a comparison between the tiny skirts and skin-tight tops of teenagers and those of street-walking sex workers. But I bet that if those same critics opened up their teenage photo albums they'd find the same so-called hooker-wear proudly on display. I've seen photos of my mum and her sisters as teenagers and they're wearing skirts so short

that I can't believe someone didn't write an editorial about the improper influence of Twiggy. Chances are your parents have similar pics stashed in a drawer somewhere.

~

Take a stand

I believe that parents have real and valid concerns about hyper-sexual media and marketing. And I feel that most of us have fair and reasonable expectations. For instance, I don't have a problem with little girls wearing singlet tops – but I do have a problem with them wearing singlet tops featuring slogans such as 'Porn Star' or 'Tease'. And make no mistake, these are real examples of girls' clothing. You've seen this kind of thing, right?

I believe we need government regulations that force advertisers and the media to act more responsibly. Yet we all need to take responsibility rather than play victim to the vile marketers and product developers who want our little sisters to go straight from Play-Doh to pole dancing. After all, girls and parents are the ones asking for, and buying, this stuff.

There are parents out there dressing their pre-teen daughters like life-size Bratz dolls. Some little girls are being put in padded lacy bras before they need a bra at all, or in shirts with slogans like 'Flirt'. Kids are wearing items from the Bratz clothing range, copied straight from the dolls' wardrobes. This marketing monster has spun off into everything from real-life hyper-sexualised clothing to stationery and make-up, including gaudy eye shadows and fake leopard-print-tipped fingernails for girls five years and over, marketed as 'everyday glam'.

I don't think parents should look surprised when girls at 13 want to dress in clothes like the ones they have been giving them to dress their dolls (and themselves!) in for years. If society passively buys into the sexualisation of children – let alone if we actively encourage it with the clothes and toys we buy girls – how can we possibly condemn those girls who do 'go wild' and pose on their Facebook pages in lingerie?

Like many little girls, my daughter used to do dancing – until one year at the annual Christmas concert I began feeling sick as I watched all the pint-size dancers dressed up and made up, like JonBenét Ramsey mini beauty queens. I had chosen Teyah's dance school as the teacher did not pressure the girls to be super-thin. Yet still, there was no escaping the hip wiggles and suggestive dance moves . . . on tiny tots. 'Aren't they cute?' many parents exclaimed. *Have we all gone insane?* I thought.

The clincher for me came after a routine based on the Austin Powers movies. A teenage girl in a long blonde wig and tiny shorts and midriff top did a super-sexy solo while the primary-school-aged mini Austin Powers boy dancers drooled on. Afterwards, the MC made a joke about the act waking up all the dads. Actually, all the dads near me looked deeply embarrassed through the routine: where to look? What to say? I wondered about the other little girls, such as my daughter who at the time was only seven, who sat watching in the wings, admiring the older girl during her routine. What messages did they take home that day about what it takes to get noticed?

Child beauty pageants like those seen on the American show *Toddlers & Tiaras* take it to a whole other level. I joined Pull the Pin, a campaign that was started by one of Enlighten Education's presenters, Catherine Manning, to try and stop that type of pageant from becoming part of Australian culture. I don't think little girls should be primped, waxed and fake-tanned to look like women, then sent out to be judged against a narrow definition of beauty. It breaks my heart to look at the pictures of the contestants. In some, the girls are heavily Photoshopped. It isn't just that they don't look like children any more but that they don't even look *real* any more.

Despite widespread community outrage, pageant organisers will still keep trying to set up these competitions, because they can make a lot of money from parents paying the entry fees. I really can't see advertisers and broadcasters backing off and ceasing to sexualise children, either. Sex sells – yes, even to little girls.

That means we simply must be more vigilant.

Amanda Gordon, President of the Australian Psychological Society, offers this advice: 'I tell parents,

'vigilant' = wary, watchful

"Don't buy sexy clothes for your children." There's nothing smart about having a four-year-old in a little bra. It's time for adults to take a stand, for parents to take a stand and say "This is what we want for our children" instead of children saying "This is what I want for me."

'... If the message is that you should be sexy and grown up, instead of being a kid, then kids aren't practising and learning how to be whole human beings ... They are instead only imitating adult behaviour, without understanding it, and that's very dangerous for their development.'

Amanda was talking to parents but I'm asking you to think about this advice when you're out shopping for your little sisters — and even for yourself.

Grow up on your own terms

There *are* alternative voices and role models of sexuality to those you see in the media and in porn. And I believe you *can* make sense of the mixed messages you are presented with.

Through my work, I meet girls and mothers who give me plenty of hope. I got to know a wonderful 11-year-old girl at a school I was at and also her mother, who completed one of Enlighten's courses for adults. The little girl was told by her dance teacher to start wearing not just full make-up for her concerts but false eyelashes, too. When her mother questioned why this was necessary, she was told by the dance teacher that the eyelashes would increase her daughter's confidence. Mum and Ms Enlightened Tween both said no. As is so often the case, the dance teacher tried making Mum feel stupid: 'But all the other parents think it's fine.' When Mum investigated this claim, she found that four out of the ten dance mothers were also worried about the appropriateness of wearing false eyelashes but had been scared to speak out.

Whether you think the eyelashes were harmless or harmful is immaterial. What I love is that this little girl will not allow herself to be stretched and pulled into becoming a 'curvy, cool teen'.

She'll be a teen who will set boundaries, deconstruct all the mixed messages she'll be presented with and make choices she is truly comfortable with. She will not allow her sexuality to be shaped by misogynistic music, plastic dolls, plastic women or the media, which would have her believe that to be hot she needs more make-up and fewer clothes.

She'll grow up on her own terms.

That is my wish for her. That's my wish for you, too.

That is what we all need to work towards.

Action plan

Ask an adult you trust and feel comfortable with to speak with you honestly and non-judgementally about sex and your own sexuality. Your school will provide information on personal development and sexuality but it is great to have significant others in your life – ideally your parents if you can talk to them – involved in this dialogue, too.

Keep in mind that the onset of puberty will unfold over many years. There is no need for you to know *everything* all at once.

And don't stress if you don't get your period until after your friends. Some girls (like me!) start menstruating much later. I didn't get my first period until I was 15 years old. I was the last within my circle of friends, and by then, even my younger sister was a menstruation veteran (oh the indignity!). You've never seen a teen girl more prepared for puberty action. I had been carrying tampons in my schoolbag for so long I think they may well have passed their use-by date! I had even had practice in breaking the news to a parent, as my best friend had been too embarrassed to tell her mother so I had broken it to her: 'Mrs Manton, our Janelle has become a woman . . .'

When I did get my period, the main feeling I had was relief. Finally, I was in the 'big girls' club! I was so elated I ran into my school assembly and screamed out, 'I have my period!' to my friends – not realising that the teachers were already present and waiting to start. My Year Advisor was very gracious and began the assembly by congratulating me. Good times.

And yes, I realise that if you are not as crazy as I am there may be a few awkward moments when you're having one of these 'special talks'. I have had these talks with girls during my time as a teacher and as a parent, too!

Be willing to attempt to resolve differences of opinion on sexuality, or at least be prepared to hear your parents or teachers out. If you don't agree with their views, put forward your opinion respectfully and see if you can get a healthy debate going. You and the person you're talking to will both learn that way. (Disclaimer: if you get sent to your room for arguing, don't blame me! I said 'healthy debate'!)

Discuss the emotional component of sex with an adult you trust, too. I always ask girls to think twice before making black-and-white statements such as 'Sex is only for people who really love each other.' Ideally, that might be true, but the reality may be quite different. Sex may be an expression of love, but it may also be an expression of boredom, curiosity, lust or even dark emotions such as anger or hate – for girls as well as boys.

I have met girls who engaged in sexual acts only to later feel embarrassed by them. By developing your own emotional vocabulary, you will learn that sex not only has obvious physical consequences – pregnancy, sexually transmitted diseases – but also an emotional impact. The glossy ads and catchy song lyrics rarely discuss complex human emotions. We should.

Deconstruct the media. The things that interest you can be tools to help you explore sexual stereotypes. Try looking at song lyrics, movies, television shows and teen magazines from a critical angle and get a discussion going with your friends or family.

> I find that when I read teen magazines I get a bit confused, as the advice offered can be quite contradictory. It's like they might say in one article that there's no rush to worry about boys and in another they go on about how to tell if a guy likes you, or show girls looking all sexy with their boyfriends.
>
> I like being able to ask my mum what she thinks, too . . . it's not as embarrassing if I can show her an article and then start talking about it, as it is when I have to try to find a way of starting the whole conversation myself.
>
> Lucy, 14

Be a positive role model. Have you bought into raunch culture? Have you accepted the myth that a woman is sexiest if she has porn-star fake boobs and can channel her inner stripper and talk about her sexual conquests? The 'girls gone wild' view of female sexuality is not always empowered or liberated. Most women in porn look vacant and bored when performing. They are not aroused. They are often not even given real names. They are not some-bodies – just bodies. They exist only to please others. Why should you emulate this? If you clearly demonstrate a healthy and self-respecting sexuality, you'll be encouraging others to respect you, too.

Reassure your little sisters (your actual little sisters if you have any, and all the other young girls who look up to you). Let them know you think the media are trying to make girls grow up too fast and that you find it unacceptable and will be working on stopping its impact on her. Girls I work with love it when I tell them that I am mad as hell and I'm not taking it any more! They love to feel protected and tell me they are deeply comforted by knowing there are women who care passionately about their wellbeing.

Care about the issue. High school girls are often furious when I show them inappropriate children's toys, and sexualised images and stories from tween magazines. In fact, at one school I worked at in Canberra, the 14-year-old girls started spontaneously booing when I showed an image of a Bratz Babyz doll! I love this anger, as it shows me that you can clearly recognise what is unacceptable for younger girls. Once you harness your outrage, you will begin to notice more examples of adult sexuality being imposed on little girls and teens – and you will be in a better position to make conscious choices about what you buy, watch and read. Get mad, girlfriends!

Connect with other like-minded girls. You might be surprised at just how many other young women share your concern over the sexualisation of children. You are not part of a moral minority! Make no mistake, outrage is widespread and mainstream. Join groups who meet in person or online. My blog (enlighteneducation.edublogs.org) can be a starting place, as it gives a voice to many people who are worried about this issue. Enlighten Education's Facebook page is also another great online community to join. You can connect with others and find information on what you can do to help the sisterhood.

Speak up. Write to companies that pressure you and your little sisters to be too sexy too soon, and tell them to *back off*. Vow not to buy their products or services unless they change their marketing campaigns or pull inappropriate items from their shelves. On the other hand, offer emails and letters of support to companies that keep it age appropriate.

Don't buy hyper-sexualised toys, clothes and other merchandise for yourself, your little sisters or your friends.

Just don't, okay? No good can come from this.

Affirmations

I am in control of my own sexuality.
I set my own boundaries and my own terms.

3

Planet Girlfriend: The Highest Highs, the Lowest Lows

How I loved my girlfriends when I was a growing up. I still do love them but the need for their company and acceptance was so very *urgent* back then.

My childhood best friend, Janelle, was in my class throughout the last few years of primary school and right throughout high school, too. Remarkably, she retained her status as my best friend the whole time (apart from a few brief periods when she was relegated to Public Enemy Number 1!). We met when we were ten years old and I had just moved into a house in the next street from hers. She approached me on the first day at my new school and declared that as I had moved into her old best friend's house and we would now be neighbours, I would need to be her new best friend. She told me she would be over at 3.30 to play.

And we did not stop playing for the next ten years.

Our friendship was initially so simple. We shared a mutual love for collecting novelty erasers, starting secret clubs (I always ensured I was the captain) and riding our bikes. We also shared my younger sister, Chantielle, who joined in all our adventures. Sure there was competition – over who had the most rubbers or who spent too much time talking to Chantielle – but it was all generally pretty uncomplicated.

By the time we hit high school, we were no longer simple little girls. Our interest shifted from exotic stationery to The Electric Pandas, an Australian rock group whose one real hit was the song 'Big Girls'. The lyrics (that I knew for definite) included 'And now we are big girls . . . I remember the days when we thought our love would never die.' Sounded like an anthem for the sisterhood to me. I never quite knew what the other lyrics were, possibly something about 'Our faces break up,' or was it actually 'We're gonna face this break-up'? As I was just starting to get pimples, I sung the former lyrics – and loved the empathy I thought the lead singer showed, not only for my love for my friends, but also for my emerging spots.

∽

The highest highs

Friendships between teen girls can be amazingly beautiful and authentic. Many girls deeply love their friends and these friendships provide a sense of belonging and acceptance that is sadly sometimes missing at home, where everyone seems to be so time poor and over-scheduled. I love the way girls giggle together, the way they play with each other's hair and cuddle, the way they can be so fiercely loyal and protective of each other. When I ask girls who it is that really knows them, understands them and loves them, the vast majority tell me it is their friends who make them feel these essential emotions of love and empathy.

A strong friendship can make you feel like you're floating, even in your darkest times.

Laura, 14

I love my friends so much. They really GET me. They understand me, accept and know me. I can be myself with them, which is a relief 'cause I am not always myself for others.

Meagin, 14

My friends are my safety. They've got my back. They won't let anyone disrespect me or hurt me and if I need anything — like, at any time — I just call them and they're there. I can call them

at midnight, at three in the morning, whenever;
it doesn't matter. We're just tight and that's it.
They're my sisters.

Ricky, 16

I love my female friends because I can talk about
anything with them. We can talk about things
that I would never bring up with my mum.

Aimee, 15

Something that I love about my female friends
is that no matter what, you can always talk to
them and even when you are smiling they always
know when something is wrong. Basically, without
them there would be no way that I could live.

Carly, 16

Truth be known, the intensity of the love girls feel for their best friends threatens some of us mothers. It can be hard to all of a sudden feel less needed and to be the third wheel. *Why won't she go out with me any more?* we wonder. *We used to be so close, now she only ever confides in her friends.*

Although you still love and need your parents, this is a time when you will be exploring what it feels like to love and need others, too. Adolescence is also the time of emerging independence and this takes the form of moving away, coming back, moving away, coming back . . . This is why you might find you adore hanging with your mum one minute and want her to leave you alone the next!

The lowest lows

Janelle and I loved 'The Pandas' so much we even had their name embroidered on sloppy joes, which we wore everywhere. On the back, we labelled ourselves as 'Big Girls'. We now had a mutual desire to be older. And to be popular. Having lots of friends was visible recognition of our value. Having one close friend no longer seemed enough. We wanted *everyone* to love us.

How to acquire new intimate friendships? We both soon developed another hobby: collecting other girls' secrets. In high school, all girls learn that knowledge is power. True?

We joined a wider circle of girls who were much cooler than we were. These girls were the 'A' group at our school. They were popular with the boys at the school next door and were slightly intimidating to the rest of us, as the leader was 'naughty'. Janelle and I knew instinctively that to maintain our position within this circle, we had to collect and disclose girl thoughts.

Once, Janelle joined the other girls in this group in forming a 'We hate Dannielle' club. I am not sure why I 'promiscuous' = having many sexual partners

was on the outer this particular week (probably I had been too bossy; I confess that I did do a lot of bossing people about in my youth) but I do recall feeling deeply betrayed, sad and lonely.

As we knew each other's secrets, my dark fears were used against me: 'You're a fat mole/slut/scrag.' Nothing worries a teenage girl more than being called fat or promiscuous, does it? It didn't matter that the insults were groundless. I was a skinny, gangly creature and although I longed for a real proper boyfriend, I was terrified of making actual contact.

I am certain that at other times, I would have betrayed Janelle and delighted in attacking her weaknesses, the weaknesses that only I knew. If need be, we were prepared to betray each other to gain wider acceptance. When at war, nothing is off limits. We could, and would, turn on each other – viciously. Hell hath no fury like a teen girl scorned . . . by another teen girl.

And then the next week, we were all friends again. If anything, the friendships seemed heightened by the drama. Like lovers reunited after a fight, we basked in the warmth of our rekindled mutual affections.

The rules on Planet Girlfriend

This on-again-off-again, happy and now sad, love her and now hate her, time for adolescent girls is governed by rules and codes that to outsiders can seem almost impossible to follow. Within girl world itself, however, the rules are generally well known and understood. Even when my friends collectively turned on me, I recall thinking that it was just the way of things, that it was simply my turn to be pushed away.

I turned then to my 'B' circle of friends, a group of girls who were not quite as cool but were very funny and smart. In hindsight, they were girls I had much more in common with and, better yet, they seemed to accept me flitting in and out of their world. This outer circle of friends had its own rules and when I dropped in to visit, it always took me some time to adjust to the new environment. I had to learn the native customs and reacquaint myself with the different language.

Each girl group has its own dress code, rules about what behaviour is acceptable and social rules that dictate whom the members can talk to and where they can sit in the school playground. Then, there are the more flexible rules that may change within the group from day to day: rules such as what it is okay to eat, watch and listen to. If you don't keep up with these rules, you can find yourself branded out of touch by your friends, doing something that is 'so yesterday'.

'hierarchy' = classification of groups of people based on their social or economic position

As we all long for connection and belonging, keeping up with the rules may seem like vital work – and it's exhausting. In my 'A' group, failing to attend a sleepover was social suicide, because back at school on Monday you would be left floundering, unable to share the in-jokes or fully comprehend the new intimacies formed between group members.

Barbie bitches and cyberbullies

'clique' = an exclusive, closed circle of people

With its cliques, secrets, passive–aggressive exchanges and tears, teen-girl world can be a political, intense place. Unlike boys, who often get physical and then forget and forgive their differences, girls tend to isolate their enemies and use words as weapons.

This can be scarring and damaging in the long term. Many women I speak to still vividly recall the pain of being teased by other girls. And they still feel guilty about teasing other girls. Often, a girl is bullied one minute and the bully the next, as she jostles for position within her social hierarchy.

The occasional falling-outs I endured were nothing

compared to the daily attacks some girls are subjected to. As a teacher, I witnessed some truly devastating episodes of girl bullying. I have seen girls' lives made miserable by their peers. Often the reasons behind this victimisation are bewildering. One girl I met in my work with Enlighten sat scribbling furiously on her feedback form at the end of the workshop. As she left the room, she hugged me — for a long time. Later, I read her comments, which included this insight into her version of Planet Girlfriend:

> I learnt today that I am beautiful and I'm not ugly because they (the other girls at my school) might say I am. I'm not what people may say I am. I can imagine, I can love, I am beautiful, I also have purpose . . .

When I asked her teachers what this girl's experience of school was like, they told me that ever since she began high school she had been tormented: pushed down stairs, spat on, ignored. Why? The other girls all thought her ears stuck out. For this girl, there was no best friend to fall back on. For this girl, there was no 'A' group, no 'B' group. No opportunity to feel connected.

Girls' hostility can escalate into a systematic campaign of verbal and physical violence. To cement her position of power, a popular 'queen bee' might get her friends to bully or hurt other girls. Then there are the 'Barbie bitches', gangs of girls who believe they are beautiful, popular and have the right to intimidate those they deem less worthy. Have you met girls like this at your school?

A study by a group of Australian academics found that as many as 93 per cent of school students had experienced some form of bullying via mobile phone. The ability to bombard someone with bullying text messages and send humiliating photos and videos to up to hundreds of other children in an instant can make this type of bullying more damaging than the older forms that your mum grew up with, such as gossip, poison-pen letters and graffiti. And text bullying is immediate. There is little time for the bully to reflect between keying in their message and hitting 'send'.

A similar study found that three out of every five young people had been bullied online. The anonymity of cyberbullying means that children who may not be capable of being physical bullies can now actively participate. My stepdaughter Jaz refers to people who are nasty online but quite meek in real life as 'keyboard warriors'. I love this term – it says it all, doesn't it? So tough when they are hiding behind their screens . . .

I tell parents and schools that banning mobile phones and the internet is not the answer. The answer is to help you develop strategies for making healthy friendships, resolving conflicts and dealing with bullies – stay tuned for tips below.

Friendship 101

Adolescence is a stage, not a lifelong condition. The brain is undergoing dramatic changes. Many of these changes start occurring in late primary school and this is when you might have started to notice girl bullying and playground drama.

The biggest brain changes relate to romantic motivation, sexual interest, emotional intensity, sleep regulation and appetite. There is also a general increase in risk-taking, novelty-seeking and sensation-seeking.

The frontal lobes of our brains are responsible for helping us to plan, consider, control our impulses, make good decisions and be empathetic. Studies into the brain development of teens have shown that your frontal lobes are not yet fully developed. Teenagers' brains 'are all tuned up for emotions, fighting, running away and romance but not so well tuned up for planning, controlling impulses and forward thinking', according to clinical psychologist Andrew Fuller.

When I was 14, a friend bit me on the arm one day, completely out of the blue. I ended up in tears, as she actually drew blood. When I asked her why she did it, she said she simply couldn't help it. I had just looked so delicious to her and she wanted to know how it would feel to bite me.

She may have *looked* 14 going on 18, yet her impulse control was non-existent. In many ways, she was just as impulsive as a toddler. It was this friend who was our 'queen bee' – wild, reckless, exciting, hilarious. No wonder she was often in trouble at school; she had little self-control. Looking back, it troubles me that our teachers did not support her to make better decisions or give her strategies to cope with her whirlwind emotions.

As a direct result of your stage of brain development, much of your behaviour is emotionally driven. I understand that your world can feel like it's crumbling if things aren't right between you and your friends.

> Arguments with friends can stuff up a whole day for me . . . If one of my friends treats me meanly, I feel guilty and think I have done something to offend them, which distracts me and stops me from thinking clearly at school.
>
> Frances, 17

> When you have positive relationships with your friends and family, it's a lot easier to succeed and be confident in what you're doing.
>
> Nicola, 15

The fact that the teenage brain is rapidly developing helps explain some of the bad behaviour girls inflict on each other, but it doesn't excuse nastiness and bitchiness. They must be called for what they are: unacceptable behaviour.

But I know lecturing you on the need to treat others with respect will not work. Nor will simply demanding more socially acceptable behaviour from girls. The development of healthy, fulfilling friendships is vital for your ongoing psychological and social development. But who shows you how to navigate girl world? Where are you supposed to learn how to deal with your complex emerging friendships? You need real, practical skills.

Let's go back to basics and take the time to learn how to make friends. Isn't it startling that this is something people are rarely shown how to do? Young people say one of their greatest needs is a sense of belonging, particularly in the middle years of school. The importance of friends cannot be underestimated. As obvious as some of these pointers may sound, it's worth reviewing them.

Making friends

1 Introduce yourself and remember names. This shows people you have seen them and taken the time and energy to notice them. I am hopeless at remembering people's names, so I make sure when I first meet someone that I say their name at least once straightaway to help me learn it: 'Hey Melinda, it is great to meet you. Melinda, how do you know Cath?' See what I did just there? Sneaky, huh?

2 Figure out who you want to be friends with and why. By doing this you will then be less likely to get caught up with friends who are not healthy for you.

Don't hide your real self from others. It's just going to lead you to people you have nothing really in common with. Don't be afraid to be yourself, either, because only then can you make a long-lasting friendship.

Brooke, 15

3 Get involved in after-school activities. This will not only help you learn new skills, it's also a great way to meet like-minded girls. Try sports teams, debating, drama and so on, until you find the right fit. I met so many hilarious people through drama at my school. And I ended up with one of the lead roles in our school production of *Wind in the Willows*. I was Mole. Yep, Mole. You're right, I did get teased for this ('Hey! You're a Mole!') but I thought Mole was such a cute, loyal little dude that I held my head up high and convinced everyone this was the coolest role. Ever.

4 Work on good conversation skills so you get better at listening and talking.

5 Don't be afraid to be positive and upbeat. Some girls might think it makes them look cool when they walk

around saying how 'lame' things are but it usually just
makes them look whiny. Agree?

6 Be sensitive to other people.

*Treat others how you would like to be treated. If
you want a good friend, start being one!*

Chelsea, 17

7 Take compliments politely and give them sincerely.
Many girls struggle with this. I am always saddened
when I compliment a girl and she responds with a
'Oh no, I am not really . . .' or 'Yes, but I am hopeless
at . . .'

8 Be willing to risk rejection. It is possible that someone
you approach may not be willing to make a new
friend. You need to be prepared for the possibility and
not take it personally. Their loss, right?

When it all goes wrong

Once you have made friends, what should you do when
things go wrong? (And things will go wrong.) Too often,
girls avoid dealing with conflict with their friends, as they
are so determined to be seen as 'nice' and nice girls don't
make a scene. Yet often all this repression does is allow
bad feelings to build up.

News flash: it is normal to have disagreements and to fall out with friends. It does not mean you are unloved or unvalued. It just means that an issue has arisen between you and your friends that needs to be resolved.

Sometimes the adults in teen girls' lives read too much into their tensions with friends. They unknowingly validate the drama by discussing it at great length and counselling girls through matters they could easily deal with themselves. A Year 6 teacher told me she would end up in tears over how unkind the girls, aged 12 to 13, were to each other. She spent nearly all her lunch hour talking to the various factions. Most of the arguments were over silly things, she said, such as who spoke to whom, or who used whose pencils. I couldn't help but think that all the special talks at lunchtime in the teacher's office may actually have been feeding this monster.

I doubt that a teacher would become emotional over boys arguing. Their fights are more often dismissed as 'boys being boys'. Is it fair that girls are expected to always be passive and nice? Due to all the changes you are experiencing in your brain and in your hormones, some anger is inevitable. And healthy! Learning how to resolve conflict in fact prepares you for coping in the big wide world. If you don't learn how to negotiate, solve problems and resolve conflict, how will you cope with everyday adult life?

The following 10 Steps to Conflict Resolution will

teach you how to deal with conflict respectfully. They are based on the respect rules set out in the excellent book for teens *Respect: a girl's guide to getting respect and dealing when your line is crossed* by Courtney Macavint and Andrea Vander Plimyn.

The 10 Steps to Conflict Resolution

1 **Plan ahead.** If you do not take the time to think about what you want to say to the person who has upset you, you may well say something you will regret ('Oh I wish I hadn't said that!') or leave out a point you really wanted to express ('Oh, I should have said that!'). This doesn't mean you need to prepare a whole PowerPoint presentation on what your friend did wrong, but talk through your feelings with someone whose opinion you value – perhaps Mum or Dad, your favourite teacher, sports coach . . .

2 **Don't put on a show.** It may be tempting to get other friends involved when you speak with the person who has upset you, but an audience will only escalate things, as everyone's emotions will be running high. A one-on-one conversation is always preferable, but if you are really fearful about confronting the other girl, you may take a support person. This person should be someone both of you feel comfortable around, and their role is merely to be an observer.

3 **Home in on how you feel.** Using 'I' language – e.g., 'I felt hurt that you talked about me to the rest of the group' – is less likely to provoke than 'you' language – e.g. 'You can't be trusted.' Develop your emotional literacy by building up a vocabulary to help you get in touch with your feelings. For example, ask yourself whether what you're feeling is really anger or betrayal. Are you scared? Threatened? Sad? Brainstorm emotions with someone you trust.

4 **Admit your mistakes and apologise.** Often all it takes to defuse the situation is for the other person to hear a simple, 'I was wrong, I am sorry.' Give an apology if you know that you are even partly at fault. A good apology should also includes a statement about what you are going to do to make amends or what you will do differently in the future.

5 **Be specific.** It is tempting to generalise and exaggerate. But it is rare that someone always does something we don't like. Clearly articulate exactly what upset you on this particular occasion and don't dig up old wounds. 'I was hurt when after the party you told Melissa that I was no longer your friend' works much better than 'You always talk about me and this is just like what you did to me in Year 6.'

6 **Offer time.** It is wise to offer the other person time to think, so that they do not speak impulsively. Try

saying something along the lines of 'I'd like to talk to you about what happened at the party as I'm feeling sad

'assertive' = bold and confident in speech and action

about how it ended. Can we talk after school, when you've had time to think about what happened, too?'

7   **Be calm.** I know, I know . . . easier said than done! Most of us get worked up when discussing friendship tensions. It is a good idea to learn and practise some simple breathing and visualisation activities that can help you to stay chilled. You can find these in the Resources section at the back. (I think of everything, don't I?)

8   **Assert yourself.** As a teacher, I learnt very quickly the difference between assertive and aggressive. If you get aggressive with a girl, she will get defensive, angry and hostile. Rightly so!

If you want the other girl to listen to you, you need to be assertive. Speak firmly and clearly, and show through your tone of voice and body language that you expect attention. Choose your words carefully and be strong in your dialogue. Try not to begin your sentences with unassertive phrases such as 'I may be wrong, but . . .' or use American pop-culture terms that detract from the power of what you're saying: 'It's kind of, like . . .' or 'When you do that, I get sort of upset and stuff'. Examples of assertive phrases you can use include: 'I don't like it when you say/do that' and 'I expect you to treat me with respect.' (Doesn't that sound oh-so-Amazon-like?)

9 **Expect to be heard.** When you approach a friend to discuss something that is important to you, you have the right to expect that friend to stop what they are doing and listen. It is reasonable for you to ask someone to put down their mobile phone or to stop looking at other things when you are speaking with them – unless you have picked a bad time to talk, in which case you should offer them time. 'I can see you're busy now but this is really important to me and I'd like your full attention. I'm happy to talk later – when suits you?'

10 **End on a positive.** Drum roll, girls . . . you do not need to be friends with everyone. Some friendships do end. However, just because a friendship ends, it does not mean that the former friend now must automatically become an enemy. It is okay to decide the friendship is over and simply move on – no longer friends, but still friendly. Also, friendships may end, but not forever. The friendship may just be 'over' for that week, or that term, or that year.

The 10 Steps to Conflict Resolution are worth using in conflicts with your parents, too.

❧

Action Plan

Set limits. If your friends practise or value behaviour that doesn't make you feel comfortable – such as bitching about others or binge drinking – then you must take a stand.

> *Don't be afraid to stand up to your friends. You soon figure out the real ones from the fake ones; the people who matter and the people who don't.*
>
> Hannah, 16

Fact: you become like the people you hang around. I am a great believer in setting boundaries early on, because the standard you walk past is the standard you set. In other words, the first time you see or hear something that does not work for you, you need to say so!

Worst-case scenario, your pals will think you have strong values that are different to theirs – which is the truth anyway. Best-case scenario, they may rethink what they are doing or saying. Either way, I bet at least a few girls in the group will respect you for saying something.

Widen your circle. I know you totally love your BFFs but be open to making new friends, too. That way, if things turn ugly in the playground, you will still have other friends you can connect with. Try sporting clubs, drama or art classes, dance schools or organised groups such as the Girl Guides.

'platonic relationship' = when you are purely friends with someone and there's nothing romantic going on

Develop friendships with boys, too. Many teen girls I know form genuine, mutually fulfilling platonic relationships with boys.

One of my closest friends is a guy. I get annoyed when my parents tease me about this or imply there is more going on. There isn't. He is attractive, I guess, but to me – he is just my buddy. And he makes me feel understood. Things with him are often less complicated than with my girlfriends . . . There isn't the same sense of competition.

Kim, 15

It is important not to make the quest for friends a popularity contest. A few good friends may be all you need, so don't be concerned if you do not have loads of close friends. I recall getting really caught up in the popularity competition when I was 14. I kept a diary that year and reading back over my thoughts is hilarious to me now! Check out this March entry: 'My goal for next month: To be popular.' My strategy centred around creating my own club:

March 13th – We decide to have a Club! It will be called The Aussie 4! We spent all day doing up the cubby house ready for it. I will be the Captain.

My goals didn't change much that year, although I did branch out: I wanted to be popular with boys, too. My goal for July?

To meet some boys and to be more popular. I love, love, love boys! But none like me! And I am scared of them! Problem!

If you think my love for boys is a bit intense, think yourself lucky you don't have to read through the many entries on my other great infatuation – novelty erasers. I collected these with a unique and somewhat frightening passion. (I still have my collection of rubber ice-creams, flowers, toilets, calculators ... I get very anxious if my children want to touch them. They are kept on a high shelf in my wardrobe and shall be my legacy to the world.) Here are some diary entries from January alone:

6th – Drove up to my Aunty's. Tops as I got some rubbers on the way!
10th – Mum bought me a $2 Instant Lotto and I won $2! I bought 4 rubbers!
18th – Bought some very cheap but very good rubbers

You get the picture.

My erasers were even the cause of a friendship fight with my bestie:

June 14th – I was so slack to Janelle as I said Simon Townsend's *Wonder World* [a popular after-school TV show] is going to film my rubber collection and interview me and I will be on TV. This is a lie. She was really hurt but she forgave me luckily.

If only I could have found a boy who loved erasers, too!

Learn to distinguish a falling-out from bullying. My diary not surprisingly catalogues a few other friendship dramas, too.

April 15th – Worst day of my entire life. Louise etc all wrote me a letter and said they hate me plus they are now playing with my other friends so I have NO ONE! I don't even know why this is happening to me!

We were all friends again two days later.

I know it can feel like the world is against you but do try to distinguish between a temporary falling-out with a friend and a real, ongoing campaign of bullying. Even today there are still some people who think bullying is just harmless name-calling. We need to get real – bullying is serious. It takes numerous forms:

+ verbal – name-calling, teasing, verbal abuse, humiliation, sarcasm, insults, threats
+ physical – punching, kicking, scratching, tripping, spitting
+ social – ignoring, excluding, alienating, making inappropriate gestures
+ psychological – spreading rumours, glaring, hiding or damaging possessions, malicious texts, email messages or Facebook comments, inappropriate use of camera phones

All are very damaging.

Bystanders need to do more to stop bullying. Think about the video that did the rounds on YouTube of a teen boy, Casey Heynes, throwing another boy to the ground in retaliation for bullying. Casey had been subjected to bullying for years and tried to turn the other cheek – until on this day, in his own words, he 'snapped'.

I was disturbed that many in the media portrayed Casey as a hero for fighting back. *A Current Affair* said he had 'finally stood up for himself', as though up until then he'd been somehow morally weak and that the only true way to stand up for yourself is to use physical force.

I empathise with the boy who had been bullied,

victimised and assaulted repeatedly before retaliating. But I think if we want to use the word 'hero', we should look at the girl at the end of the video. After the assaults, a friend of the bully comes forward to stop Casey from assaulting the bully. Then a girl walks over and stands between them and assertively tells the bully's friend to back off.

One of the things that alarmed me in that video was the number of bystanders doing nothing or, worse still, filming the violence. Like I said earlier, the standard we walk past is the standard we set. That girl was amazing. The fact that she came forward to stop the violence in a nonviolent way is to be celebrated – and encouraged in all schools. *She is an Amazon.*

Teachers are of course responsible for doing everything they can to stop bullying – but the reality is that in 85 per cent of cases, bullying takes place when there are no adults around. That's why it is so important that bystanders step up and say, 'It's not on!'

At the time the Casey Heynes video made headlines, I was asked by the media to discuss what young people who are being bullied can do about it. I asked the police youth liaison officer at Castle Hill in Sydney, Senior Constable Rob Patterson, for his input. He told me that his number one piece of advice to kids who are being bullied is: '*Tell* someone, and if they don't listen, *tell* someone else.' I think this is incredibly important advice.

If you are being intimidated or harassed, speak out. Yell if you need to!

'ostracise' = to banish or exclude someone from a group

Assess your relationships with your friends. Are you caught up in any toxic girl friendships? Do you have any friends who belittle you, dismiss you or make you feel ostracised? Or do you think you might be doing that to others? If so, it's time to free yourself of these patterns and choose healthier friendships. No one needs a frenemy.

Celebrate good friendships. For many of you, girlfriends are some of the most important people in your lives. I find it sad that the media (and some parents) mock the need you have for connection – especially when you choose to connect online. Every so often, new research is published on how much time teens are spending online and using social media. Eye-catching headlines are designed to shock: 'Teenage "hypertexters" more likely to have sex, drink, use drugs', 'Psychologist warns of Facebook dangers', 'Facebook warning after Aust teen lured to death'. I am not sure us mothers were that different in terms of wanting to hang with our girlfriends. My Program Manager for Enlighten in New Zealand, Rachel Hansen, recalls:

As a teenager, I spent many hours camped on our family landline. I would farewell my friends at school, and then as soon as I got home I would be on the phone. I have a note in my 1992 diary exclaiming: 'Broke my phone record!!! 6 hours non-stop!!! One phonecall!!!' (My mind boggles. Did we have toilet breaks? Refreshment pauses?)

And when we weren't talking on the phone, we were writing to one another. Pages and pages and pages. My friends and I would wave goodbye as we headed off to our respective classes or homes, and these waves would always be accompanied with 'Write me a letter!' When we saw each other again, we would exchange letters and keep them to read when we next had to endure separation for more than 10 minutes. Due to my hoarding tendencies, I have kept every one of these letters. And let me clarify that these are not notes — some stretch to 20 pages long!

The technology is different now but the drive is the same: the desire to connect with others, explore friend-ships, delve deeper into your emotions, and understand and develop relationships. When it comes to core needs and values, you are not that different to your mum's gen-eration as teens. It is just that the tools you use to express yourselves have changed.

Some people are concerned that social media prevents

girls from developing real friendships. Have you heard that one? In presenting Enlighten workshops to teen girls all around Australia and New Zealand, I see no evidence of this. I see girls hugging, talking and sharing their lives with one another. They write about how important their best friends are in their lives. In fact, research by Girl Scouts USA indicates that: 'despite popular perception, social networks are not necessarily a "girl's best friend" ... The vast majority of girls prefer face-to-face communication. Ninety-two per cent would give up all of their social networking friends if it meant keeping their best friend.'

The study also showed that 52 per cent of girls have used a social networking site to become involved in a cause that they care about, and more than half agree that social networking online helps them feel closer to their friends.

So there. Go send a friend you love a message. Hey, send a few!

Share. Talk to the adults in your world when you feel confused about a friendship dilemma. They won't always be able solve the problem for you, but talking it through will probably make you feel a lot better and will help you get the issues clear in your mind.

Affirmations

I surround myself with positive people and attract good friends into my life.

I have compassion, I'm a good listener and I choose my words carefully.

4

Drinks with the Girls

We are in the midst of a teen drinking epidemic. And it is girls who are overindulging the most. Studies reveal that girls aged 12 to 15 are three times more likely than boys the same age to drink alcohol at least once a week.

Over 80 per cent of the drinking done by boys and girls aged 14 to 17 is at risky levels that often lead to injury. It takes a teen longer than it takes an adult to feel the physical signs of being drunk, so teenagers tend to binge, or drink to a more dangerous level, not realising how drunk they are.

Research shows that drinking alcohol during the teen years can interrupt key stages of your development. A teenager's brain is also not yet fully developed for reasoning or thinking about consequences; it is far more finely tuned to respond to situations emotionally. Combine this with alcohol and you truly have a risky cocktail. Many girls lament regrettable decisions they have made whilst under the influence. I am sure you know stories like this.

Too many teen girls are jeopardising their safety, health and their development. They are burdening themselves with hangovers and regrets. Why?

'I kissed a girl'

There is no one reason why anyone drinks, but in the many hundreds of conversations I have had with teenage girls about their binge drinking, some common threads have emerged. I think it is important to share these with you as it will give you an insight into what might be driving some of your (or your friends') behaviours.

In our hyper-sexualised culture, there is increasing pressure on teen girls to gain attention by doing stripper-like dance moves and bare all when go out with friends. Girls tell me this is easier to do when they are drunk and therefore less inhibited.

How revealing are the lyrics to the song 'I Kissed a Girl' by Katy Perry, in which she tells of kissing a girl even though she hadn't intended to: 'I got so brave, drink in hand . . .'. It seems for Katy that the act of kissing another girl had more to do with alcohol – and a desire to provoke her boyfriend, mentioned later in the song – than any real pressing sexual urge of her own.

> 'blacking out' = drinking so much you can't recall what has happened to you

Ms Perry moved on from kissing girls to drunk group sex by the time she sang 'Last Friday Night'. In that song, despite her drunken night concluding with a stranger in her bed, bruises, photos of the threesome she had being posted online and blacking out, she decides it ruled and she wants to do it all again next week.

Teen girls tell me Katy is right – it is now almost passé to have a girl-on-girl kissing session in front of the boys at parties. One girl told me: 'Getting smashed and then getting it on with a girlfriend used to be a guarantee of getting attention at parties, but now the boys expect more. They've seen it all before. Now they're like "Yeah, yeah, whatever."'

Girls also post their drunken antics on social networking sites such as Tumblr and Facebook, or on YouTube, in the hope that they will gain instant celebrity status. It is no wonder alcohol has become a way of getting attention, given how fixated we are with celebrities behaving badly. We voyeuristically feast on the alcohol- or drug-fuelled escapades of Lindsay Lohan, Miley Cyrus, Taylor Momsen ... We inadvertently glorify their train-crash behaviour by watching fascinated as these stars are carried out of bars and night clubs, or are forced into rehab.

When teen girls publicise their drunken exploits, it has long-term implications for their lives. Just look at the media's and public's reaction to Lindsay, Miley and the gang: we may see them as celebrities but we also denigrate them as trash. Society is generally less forgiving of the 'fallen woman' than the 'man who likes a drink'. I cannot imagine that a male celebrity getting drunk, acting in an overly sexual way and passing out would capture the headlines in quite the same way as the female celebrities do.

Searching for the escape hatch

Despite the headlines that scream 'raunchy', I do not think the paparazzi photos of drunk or drugged female stars look in the least bit sexy. Yes, they flash the right pieces of their anatomy. Yes, they engage in the almost mandatory girl-on-girl grope – yet their eyes look glazed and bored. They are surrounded by hangers-on, yet they look lonely. Have you noticed that?

Lonely and perhaps sad. Drinking can be a way of self-medicating depression; bingeing is often a form of escape. Ironically, as alcohol is ultimately a depressant, girls who drink to drown their sorrows end up feeling worse ... and drinking more.

Girls also tell me they drink because they are bored. When drunk they feel more outgoing. The uncontrollable giggling, toppling over and even making themselves sick is, they say, hilarious. And it can bring them closer to their friends, they argue. Some girls will do almost anything to fit in with their peers, right?

The alcopop industry

The alcohol industry has made a big push to appeal to young female drinkers' tastes. Prior to the early 1980s, the alcohol market included only beer, wine and spirits. Then alcopops – called ready-mixed drinks, or RMDs, by the industry – were introduced. Combinations of alcohol and fruit juices, flavourings and soft drinks, they were designed to appeal to new drinkers who did not yet find the taste of alcohol appealing.

All that sweetness masks the punch. In 2008, Australian consumer group Choice got 78 teenagers (for legal reasons all aged 18 or 19) to do a taste test of soft drinks, alcopops, wine and beer. Though they could taste the alcohol in the wine and beer samples, when comparing the alcopops and soft drinks, one in four of the teenagers could not tell which contained alcohol.

With the introduction of alcopops, getting trashed became delicious. Whether a girl wants to drink to lose her inhibitions, to forget her problems or simply to be part of the gang, thanks to alcopops she can now do so without even having to taste the alcohol.

My story

I am going to be really honest with you here (*Danni takes a big breath for courage*): as a teen girl, at various points I drank for all the reasons above. It began at 14, when my friends and I would scull oh-so-sugary-sweet Passion Pop before underage Blue Light discos run by the local police. How the police that supervised these events never noticed that more than half the teens were blind drunk, I will never know. Most of us could hardly stand, let alone dance.

Looking back now, what a sad sight we must have made. Young girls still dressed with pictures of Minnie Mouse on our shirts and jumping up with glee when our favourite song came on – smashed. We drank because everything became even more amusing. Falling over? How funny! Vomiting on your own feet? Hilarious! And we lost our social inhibitions. My diary entries from this time tell the story best:

October 15th – Pashed Scott twice but I don't love him or really care if we don't get together again. Louise F nearly died as she got so drunk the cops called an ambulance.

November 5th – Tops party! We all got so drunk. We all went for a bush walk and I fell and hit my head which was so funny! I cried as Julie went to the toilet 16 times (as she was so sick) which scared me.

I had my first meaningful kiss – with a boy I'd had a crush on for months – when I was drunk. I launched myself at him. He was drunk as well, so we sat together in a drunken embrace, no longer afraid of revealing that we liked each other. Now, to really get his attention I might feel pressured to provide him with a lap dance, too – but back then, a pash sufficed.

Later, as an older teen, I started to drink to dull my potential. My schoolgirl head ached with facts, figures, quotes for essays. It throbbed with a self-imposed pressure to be first, to be the smartest, the brightest. When I was drunk, I could barely string coherent sentences together, let alone formulate an argument. Being drunk was like taking a mind vacation.

For me, drinking seemed so grown-up, because I saw the majority of the adults around me doing it. Alcohol features significantly in many elements of Australian culture, from celebrations to commiserations. It is considered almost un-Australian not to have a beer, isn't it?

In my house, my father drank from the moment he came home from work until he collapsed, asleep. While this wasn't very appealing to watch, strangely enough, to me it did look relaxing. And he became more cheerful and animated . . . until after the fifth or sixth beer, when he just became quiet. Or violent.

I felt quite rebellious engaging in an activity that seemed so adult and also so masculine. Largely as a result

'Victim blaming' = when the victim of a crime, accident or any type of abuse is said to be partly responsible

of watching my dad in his rages – which were thankfully infrequent but still shocking and memorable – I associated being drunk with power. I knew very few women who drank heavily. Certainly none of the women in my family drank. Perhaps they may have had the occasional shandy (beer mixed with lemonade) but I never saw them drunk.

It was almost as if being young women of the post-feminist age, we saw it as our right to indulge, too. If the boys could all get hammered, why couldn't we? Girl power!

Looking back at this stage in my life, I can see how dangerous my behaviour was. Being drunk did not really make me powerful. It made me vulnerable. My academic results suffered. I said things to friends I regretted the next day. I took stupid risks when drunk that I would never have taken sober: hitchhiking, crashing out by myself in rooms at wild parties, walking home alone, getting into cars with very drunk drivers. The fact that nothing truly serious ever happened to me was more good luck than anything else.

While drinking makes people feel invincible, they are actually far more at risk when they are drunk. Their judgement is compromised; their reflexes are slowed; they are physically awkward. Girls are at greater risk of violent and sexual assaults when they are drunk. I am not blaming the victim: it is never her fault. Sadly, being drunk does make everyone an easier target. We know that predators are looking for vulnerability, so we are at increased risk when we are intoxicated. Drinking is not so much a sign of liberation from sexism as it is a new form of enslavement for many teenage girls (and for many women, too).

∽

What every girl should know about alcohol

In this section, please take into account that figures are available only for men and women over the legal drinking age, 18.

Females are more vulnerable to the effects of alcohol than males. This is because males and females are physically different and so their bodies process alcohol differently. When a person drinks, alcohol enters the bloodstream and then, being water soluble, it is distributed throughout the tissues of the body that contain water. Females usually have smaller bodies than males, which means that there is less water volume to take up the alcohol, leading to a higher concentration of alcohol in the bloodstream and a greater effect.

This is compounded by the fact that fatty tissues do not take up alcohol and females have a higher proportion of body fat than males. With fewer tissues in the body to take up the alcohol, a female will be more affected than a male who consumed the same amount. Additionally, the body's 'cirrhosis' = scarring and poor functioning of the liver, which can be caused by alcohol abuse

ability to break down and rid itself of alcohol is limited by the size of the liver and on average females have smaller livers than males.

The culture of dieting and striving to be thin also increases the impact of alcohol on females. Dieting leads to an excessive loss of body fluid and as it is the body's water content that takes up alcohol, there will be a higher concentration of alcohol in a dieter's system. This has serious implications for teenage girls.

Heavy drinking is risky for both males and females, but females are more prone to the effects of alcohol abuse. Because of our physical differences, the risk to our health starts at lower rates of alcohol consumption than it does for males. For women, the risk of premature death increases once we start drinking more than two standard drinks of alcohol a day. At that point, the risk of death climbs to 40 per cent higher than it is for non-drinkers. For men, on the other hand, the risk begins to increase at four drinks a day.

The greater the amount of alcohol a person drinks above the guidelines, the higher their risk of premature death. Hence bingeing – consuming an excessive quantity of alcohol at once – is especially dangerous.

Because our livers are smaller than men's, women are vulnerable to liver damage and cirrhosis at lower levels of alcohol consumption. Alcohol increases a woman's risk of breast cancer and the risk rises with the level of alcohol consumed. A woman who drinks three or four standard drinks a day has a 35 per cent higher risk of breast cancer than one who drinks little or none. If a woman drinks more than four standard drinks a day, her risk is 67 per cent greater.

Alcohol-related deaths in women usually take the form of strokes, injuries from falls, alcoholic liver cirrhosis, road accidents and breast cancer. Alcohol poses a further physical threat to women and girls in that it may increase the risk of being harmed by violence. There is a risk that drunkenness may lead to unsafe sex or an unplanned pregnancy; and there are also risks to the health of an unborn child. Lastly, research shows that teenagers, especially teen girls, who drink excessively are more likely to become alcoholics.

❧

Beyond bingeing

The last day I drank alcohol was years ago, at my daughter's seventh birthday party. It had been a big day. As well as the kids, there were lots of adults over and, as always, lots of adults meant lots of booze.

I spent the next day lying in bed moaning and swearing – yet again – that I would stop drinking.

How many times had I had this conversation with myself?

Was it really okay that here I was at 36, still wiping myself out?

My children, at ages five and seven, were surely becoming aware of the difference between adults who are sober and those who aren't. I wondered what they made of my drinking.

I did not start the day with alcohol and on weeknights I usually didn't have my first drink until the children had gone to bed. I never drank and drove. I had never needed a day off work due to being hung-over. The majority of my friends drank just as much as I did, just as frequently. Yet was downing a bottle of wine or more at each drinking session really okay?

No. I felt increasingly exhausted, both physically and emotionally. I was sick of looking for reasons to have a 'chardie'. I was disappointed in myself for never seeming to know when I had had enough. It saddened me that in my bright, shiny life this 'drinking thing' was a part of me. It just did not fit with the strong woman I knew was my authentic self.

I sought out a GP I could talk to who could help me make better choices. I hadn't realised how much I relied on drinking until I was committed to stopping. The first few months were gruelling and there was surprisingly little support from my girlfriends, who were still drinking. 'Why stop completely?' 'How boring, Danni!' 'We won't be inviting you over for drinks and nibbles, then.'

But I knew I could never be a restrained social drinker. I never had been. It had always been all or nothing. Perhaps I have a genetic tendency towards drinking or maybe it's because I watched my father drink so heavily at home. What I do know for sure is that my dad's drinking completely destroyed his life: he lost his job and his family. I was not going to wait for the train to crash before I jumped off!

I don't believe it is just teens who have a problem with drinking. I think it is time for adults to end unhealthy drinking, too. Teens are targeted by campaigns against binge drinking but when I speak with them, they'll tell me that though some of their peers do binge drink, it's not fair that all young people are 'tarred with the same brush' and singled out. As Jennifer Duncan reported in Brisbane's *Sunday Mail*, binge drinking is 'a whole-of-community issue' and one we all need to take responsibility for if we are to resolve it. 'The first step in the binge drinking debate,' she wrote, 'is to acknowledge what young people are learning from our own behaviour and to adjust this behaviour accordingly.'

It frightens me that many parents seemingly dismiss their teen daughters' (and sons') drinking as just a rite of passage. I have spoken to many mums and dads who are almost hysterical about the possibility their teen daughter might start using drugs or have her drink spiked with drugs, yet are not at all concerned when they hear that she has been drinking alcohol. Often parents are the ones who buy the alcohol for their teens, allow unsupervised parties and lead an alcohol-goes-with-everything lifestyle, acting as drinking role models.

How can we move forward?

Promising news came out of a teen-drinking study conducted by St Peter's Collegiate Girl's School, in Adelaide. It showed that girls are already well placed to learn new attitudes to drinking. The girls surveyed readily accepted people who did not drink alcohol, believing that they were free to choose not to drink. Across all year levels, the girls were well informed about drinking hazards such as binge drinking. The Year 12 girls felt very strongly about the role of parents in relation to underage drinking. These girls actually *wanted* enforced curfews and they did not want parents to turn a blind eye to their teens drinking. Most of the teen girls I speak with actually crave boundaries and limits, because the pressure is then taken off them to make all the decisions. True?

If limits are not being set for you, then set your own. My stepdaughter, Jazmine, 17, chose to not drink at the parties she went to in her mid-teens, even though nearly all her friends at the time were already starting to get wasted. 'At first some people did tease me a bit and said I was scared or straight . . . but after a while I just got a reputation as an individual and it was surprising how many people said they respected me for it – especially as it was always so ugly seeing girls vomiting and crying,' she says.

I have seen girls drink but I don't. I think they look stupid, out of it . . . Girls just get smashed to impress other girls. I would never do that.

Rose, 13

An example of peer pressure actually being a positive force is that if you're at a party, there is always someone there that will say you don't have to drink or you don't have to smoke.

Brooke, 14

Drinking is really common in a small country town. It's like the only thing the other girls talk about all week at school — what they drank, how smashed they were, when they will drink next. I don't drink at all, which does make it harder to fit in, but I think drinking is just so stupid. If I have fun, I want to remember it after!

Lucy, 16

❧

Action plan
Ask yourself some tough questions:

+ Do I drink too much and too often?
+ If so, what does my drinking say about how I socialise?

+ What does my drinking say about how I manage stress?

If you need help to take control of your drinking, seek it now. It will be much easier to form new habits now – trust me. Don't wait for the train to crash; get off before things get ugly. Having quit alcohol myself, I know that it may seem like an overwhelming challenge – but you don't have to go it alone. In the 'Resources' section at the back of this book you will find contact details for help, support and more information.

Consider the consequences. There are a couple of great short films made by a girl, Kylee Darcy, to dissuade other teen girls from drinking. The films won a competition in the United States that asked girls to make Public Service Announcements that showed why underage drinking wasn't worth the adverse consequences. Darcy's films portray two teen girls who become ostracised by their peers, are thrown off a sporting team and get busted by their parents when a video of one of them drinking at a party surfaces on a social networking site.

Watch the videos, at www.alot2lose.com, and then ask yourself the following questions, or discuss them with your parents or friends.

1   Have you ever seen people acting in a way they wouldn't normally, because they were drunk? How did it make you feel?

2   As well as the social risks of drinking, what physical dangers are there in drinking too much? In what ways does it make girls more vulnerable and exposed?

3   What can you do to cut these risks for you and your friends?

4   If you saw friends acting in a way that made you anxious what would you do? What could you do to take control of the situation?

5   Do you think that these films get the message across about why it's bad to binge drink? What would make them more effective or relevant to you and your friends?

Seek alternatives. Get involved in special underage drug- and alcohol-free events.

If things go wrong. If you or a friend do get drunk, be sure to increase your water intake, as you may be dehydrated. Don't leave a very drunk person alone to 'sleep it off' – they may slip into unconsciousness. And don't be afraid to get help. If someone is sick at a party, let a (sober) adult know. Call an ambulance if you are worried. Things can get quickly out of control and alcohol is the most common cause of drug-related deaths in teenagers.

Affirmations

My body is a temple and I honour it by making good, healthy choices.

I seek healing, healthy ways to relax and enjoy myself.

5

Shopping for Labels . . .
or Love?

When I was little, I fancied myself growing up to be a lawyer. I could picture myself standing up in front of a packed courtroom, everyone listening, rapt, as I upheld justice. As it turned out, my calling in life turned out to be standing not in front of judges and juries but in classrooms, talking – and perhaps more importantly, listening – to young people.

When I talk to teen girls about what they want to be when they leave school, for many it is not a question of choosing a profession such as lawyer, doctor or teacher. It is about money and fame. At high school level, I have heard the refrain: 'Don't care what I am, Miss, as long as I make money, hey?' In primary school, I have seen girls

> 'materialism' = devotion to physical objects – such as designer clothes, shoes, phones, expensive jewellery – rather than life's spiritual and emotional rewards

between six and seven years old who have goals such as 'be famous', 'be a model', 'be on TV' or 'be pretty, famous and maybe a singer and actress'.

Wanting to be a successful businesswoman or skilled professional, or to excel as an artist or entertainer, is a worthy goal. I am inspired when I see entrepreneurship and ambition in girls, because I know the freedom and sense of personal fulfilment that success in a business or career can bring. What worries me is the vagueness and materialism of wanting just to 'be rich' or 'be famous'. The message girls are being sent is that the only measures of success that truly count are fame and wealth. Not fame and wealth as a result of a specific skill, talent or course of study, just fame and wealth.

You can see it in reality TV shows that turn ordinary people who can kind of sing or are almost models into insta-celebrities dripping in cash prizes and endorsement deals for major brands. You can see it in glossy magazines that obsess over the latest hot designer must-have bag, jeans, mobile phone, party dress, boots or necklace. Fame, wealth and branded luxury products have fused into a great big seductive orb that many people are attracted to like moths to a flame.

Your generation has been found to be the most brand-aware in history. The average teenager in the United States has 145 conversations about brands each week. In the UK, almost half of children surveyed said that the only kind of job they want when they leave school is one 'that pays a lot'. In Australia, children aged 10 to 17 have 'more money, more toys and more things to spend their money on than ever before', according to the YouthSCAN national survey, which takes the pulse of the country's youth every two years.

Why should you be concerned about this? Because it means you are taking on some very adult-size burdens that teenagers never used to worry about. Australian teens are working and earning more than ever before and a significant number are suffering stress from owing money to credit card companies, mobile phone carriers, and friends and family.

They are beginning to show signs of something usually only adults suffered from: choice fatigue. That's when you become overwhelmed by the vast array of consumer products to choose from. A good example of this? When you have a 'clothing crisis' and you don't know what to wear, it can seem like there are just too many possible options. More and more kids wish that the whole consumer merry-go-round would just slow down for a second. Researchers have even found that when a child is more materialistic, she tends to be more depressed and anxious and have lower self-esteem.

Teenagers now account for a big chunk of the consumer market, so you are being ferociously targeted by marketing and advertising campaigns. While you are still learning, growing into adults and forming your identity, marketers want to turn you into loyal consumers of their brands. You can't help but feel a chill when you read the words of one marketing professional who said at a big marketing and advertising shindig in New York: 'Kids are the most powerful sector of the market, and we should take advantage of them.' Can you think of any circumstance where it's okay for the words 'kids' and 'take advantage of' to be linked? Me neither.

Right about now you might perhaps be bracing yourself for an anti-consumerist lecture. But my aim isn't to make you feel bad about getting a kick out of shopping, or to make you feel guilty for lusting after that cool new phone or cute handbag. Don't fear: I am certainly not about to give up the occasional shopping splurge. I'm not saying that shopping and spending money is *all bad*. What I am saying is that we should take a minute to look more deeply into what motivates our spending and what influences our attitudes towards money.

It's okay to want that designer bag, but first, let's unpack it ...

Designer-label armour

When I was a teenager, girls tried to distinguish themselves from the older generation. This is one area where life for you is different today: now you and your mum may well be scrabbling to snatch the same handbag in the sales. You might borrow each other's belts. I know my girls both borrow my shoes (unfortunately for me, we are all the same size!). And something may happen in your home that would have been totally alien to my mother: your mum might occasionally listen to your fashion tips!

More and more, young girls are aspiring to wear designer labels that were once associated only with grown women who read *Vogue*. At the age of five, Suri Cruise had a $150,000 designer shoe collection. *Glamour* magazine ranked her number 21 in their list of the World's 50 Best Dressed Women. She was right up there with Kate Moss and Keira Knightley. So, at five a girl is a woman now? At five she is meant to be coordinating her pumps with her purses? Pressure much?

At the same time, grown women are buying the same hot designer brands. Where once your average woman may not have known a Manolo from a Christian Louboutin, today she and her daughter may both be luxury-brand literate. The dividing line between what is fashionable for mothers and daughters has become blurry. Both groups covet a lot of the same products.

My mum loves fashion also, and knows heaps of new styles before I do . . . I often borrow my mum's clothes; I also ask her opinion on what I am wearing a lot, too. I like going shopping with my mum just as much as I do with friends, since we have very similar tastes in clothes and like shopping at the same shops, as well as liking the same labels.

Paris, 14

It's important to me to buy certain clothes, shoes, bags, phone, etc. – my mum is very understanding with that sort of thing. And I love her for it. I like going shopping with my mother because I love spending time with Mum! She's the best thing in the world.

Renee, 15

Me and my mum have similar tastes in fashion, so it makes shopping a lot more fun because on the rare occasion that we have a shopping day, we go to the same store.

Maddi, 16

For teen girls, the aim is to look more sophisticated, while for us women the goal is to look youthful. Clothes, shoes, bags, cosmetics, lotions, hair-care products, sunglasses and bling – many teens use them to craft a more adult, worldly look. With the same products (plus a stash of wrinkle serums) women do the reverse: we aim to look young and hip. Many teen girls want to look like they're in their twenties – powerful, savvy, in-the-know, sexy and rich. So do many of their mums. And this look does not come cheap. At the very least, it has to *seem* like it took a celebrity's salary to achieve it.

Rose, a 13-year-old girl I know through my work who happens to be naturally stunning, told me it takes her just over an hour to get ready for school each morning. 'I have a shower, then put on my make-up, blow-dry my hair and then straighten it . . . I wear mascara, eyeliner, lip gloss, moisturiser for my face and legs, glitter on my eyes – like, if it is a special-occasion day – deodorant and body spray. I have done this since Year 7, when I was 12.'

As Rose told me this, it struck me that she is like a warrior preparing to go to battle, slipping on her armour, piece by piece, until she feels strong and powerful and ready to go out and face the fight. Many grown women perform a similar ritual at the start of each day. It is something girls and women do to feel strong and in control. Just as the young women in *Gossip Girl* express their prestige, power and sexuality through shoes and handbags, perhaps that is what many of us are attempting to do, too. Women and girls are armour-plating themselves, outwardly expressing independence, strength and a don't-mess-with-me attitude.

Marketers capitalise on the urge you have to feel independent by infusing 'girl power' into their

'commodity' = something
that is sold or traded

products – although they define the term a whole lot differently to the way I do! Australian cosmetics guru Napoleon Perdis used girl power to sell, of all things, a lip gloss. Apparently, it was 'The Ultimate Girl Power in a Gloss'. There is actually an entire brand, Girl Power Beauty, marketing skin and hair-care products to tweens. How about a cute little T-shirt with giant glossy supermodel lips and the words 'Girl Power' emblazoned across the bust line? You can order one online now.

Marketers and department stores love it when we equate certain bags and shoes, or outward qualities such as looking fashion-savvy and hip, with female strength, independence and, ultimately, happiness. But all those women in past decades who fought against gender inequality didn't do it just so we could shop. Surely the real reason we want equal pay for women is not simply so that we can spend it on more stuff . . . *beauty* stuff.

Jennifer Thomson wrote, '"Girl Power" is feminism, but feminism by marketed, picture-perfect, precise numbers.' She was writing about the original girl-power group, the Spice Girls, whose success showed that our marketing-laden culture likes 'to turn people into things. The inventions of Baby, Sporty, et al, stripped away the person to leave behind a commodity.'

Victoria Beckham and her husband, David, embody

this. Open any glossy mag and you will probably see one of them gazing out, imploring you to buy perfume, underwear, shoes, clothes. Posh, one of the original icons of girl power, has, along with Becks, become a living brand. (And as *Glamour* ranked her number 15 on their list of the best dressed, she still out-dressed the real-world 'Baby Spice', Suri Cruise.)

For girls and women alike, marketing messages can be very seductive, as can the pictures we see splashed everywhere of the rich, famous and powerful packaged head-to-toe in brand-label products. It may seem that we will be empowered if we buy those products. They promise to signal to the world that we have prestige and status, and that we are desirable and should be taken seriously. But real girl power is not about buying products. *Things* don't make us powerful. Deep down, I think we all know that it isn't clothes, bling and the latest mobile phone that can truly make us feel happy and in control. Only we ourselves have the power to do that.

⸝⸎⸏

Standing out, fitting in

You want to be and look like an individual, with your own style and image, your own identity. Yet at the same time, no teenage girl wants to be perceived as uncool or clueless about what's in. You want to be part of a group; you 'paradox' = something that seems self-contradictory yet is true

have a genuine and valid need to fit in with your friends.

If you're too slavish a follower of the latest fashions, you might get called a try-hard. On the other hand, if you're wearing the wrong shoes you risk being relegated to the outer reaches of the girl-world galaxy. Was it just me or does everything from getting a new hairstyle to getting ready for plain-clothes days at school cause some major stress? My diary from when I was 14 reveals what these pressures felt like for me (warning, serious child-of-the-'80s alert):

July 8th – I am getting a perm. I am very worried. I HOPE it is good!

July 9th – My perm is tops! I'm in love with it, it is so nice. Everyone at school loves it.

July 19th – We had a mufti-day at school and I wore really nice pink leg warmers. Everyone said they looked very nice. I felt so happy all day!

The people who sell products to you are only too aware of this eternal teenage paradox. Owning the right brands and products – and putting them together in her own style – is one way that a teen girl can walk that razor's edge between being in and being out. Brand ownership enables a girl to associate with a group of other kids who gravitate towards those brands.

The labels and products a girl displays can be like a social code, offering up signs of what kind of girl she is and who her tribe is. For instance, a Ralph Lauren top, Tiffany charm bracelet and Burberry bag sends out one signal. Vans sneakers, Roxy cargo pants and a Billabong T-shirt sends a whole other signal, doesn't it? The importance of the social aspect of clothing can be seen when girls go shopping in packs. When a girl holds an item up to her friends and asks, 'What do you think?' she's second-guessing her own taste and testing whether it fits in with her tribe's.

In our marketing-saturated culture, product ownership has joined the list of factors girls use to rank each other socially. To a girl's beauty and popularity we can add the rating of how fashionable and prestigious the stuff she owns is.

American author Alissa Quart looked at the world of teen marketing for her eye-opening book *Branded: The Buying and Selling of Teenagers*. What she noticed during her research was that the girls who owned the most name-brand products tended to be those who struggled to fit in according to the standard criteria girls judge one another by. They were awkward or weren't conventionally attractive. 'While many teenagers are branded,' she writes, 'the ones most obsessed with brand names feel they have a lack that only superbranding will cover over and insure against social ruin.'

A lot of kids feel that products boost their self-esteem, identity and social success. More than 60 per cent of kids aged 12 to 13 said that 'buying certain products makes them feel better about themselves'. More than half of the same children felt pressured to buy particular clothes because their friends had them. In a way, it is as if marketers and advertisers that target you are selling not handbags, make-up or mobile phones, but the promise of friendship and a sense of belonging.

Formal madness

The frenzy for wearing the right labels reaches hysteria point around Year 10 and Year 12 formal time. In the lead-up, a girl's list of what she needs for the big night can become the teen equivalent of a bridezilla's: the right designer dress (actually, two dresses, one for the formal, another for the after party), jewellery, handbag and shoes, professional hair and make-up, tanning, waxing, buffing and sufficiently glamorous transport to get them there, stretch Hummers being a particular favourite.

Parents often don't mind shelling out generally well over a thousand dollars for just one night in their teenager's life. Mums get almost as excited about it as their daughters. When I was at school, formals weren't such a big deal and even if any girls were wear-

> 'vicarious' = experienced through the feelings or actions of another person

ing designer dresses, we probably didn't realise. Having missed out on the hoopla, it seems that plenty of mothers are happy to spend up big so they can vicariously experience it through their daughters. This only fuels the competitive madness of it all.

At one high school, a girl bragged to me that her mother had flown her *to Paris* to buy her formal dress. I was speechless when, in the next breath, she revealed that there was a down side: as it was a Parisian label, only diehard fashionistas would know the designer, so she would have to explain to the other girls how prestigious her dress was.

If girls harnessed all the energy they spend on what they'll look like on formal night, think of all the other great things they could achieve. They could probably light up a major city!

❧

Buying a lifestyle

Have you noticed that companies create a whole lifestyle around a brand? There are not just clothes, but also handbags, purses, shoes, sunglasses, watches, earrings, pendants, rings, gym gear, key rings, mobile phone bling, perfume, body sprays, room scents, home wares, and on and on it goes. Ads feature gorgeous, sexy, fulfilled-looking young people just hanging out together laughing (or scowling fashionably, depending on the brand) and at the end you wonder, 'Hang on, what product are they selling?' That is because it's not so much a product you are being sold as a feeling.

Girls and women are encouraged to feel a positive emotion – a sense of belonging, perhaps – when they see the brand's label. It's not that the handbag bearing this particular label is really all *that* different to any other handbag in the shops at the same time. They both do the same job: carrying your stuff. It's the emotion, the lifestyle, the identity associated with the label that makes someone want to buy that particular handbag.

If a company can capture you early on, can make you associate yourself and your lifestyle with their brand, they have a friend – oops, customer – for life. As Alissa Quart writes, 'teenagers have come to feel that consumer goods are their friends – and that the companies selling products to them are trusted allies.' Marketers openly admit that pushing a brand is all about giving the shopper a positive emotion and a sense of being connected, not just to the brand, but to the entire lifestyle and community the brand represents.

Can I be in your club?

Celebrity endorsements play a big role in selling products because fans want to belong to the same club as their favourite star. The celebrity makes the brand a star and, by extension, a person who buys that brand feels they have become a little bit of a star, too. When I ask teen girls about their ideal job, quite a few say 'celebrity stylist'. But make no mistake, 'celebrity stylist' doesn't equal 'celebrity BFF'. I am going to bet that an average day at the office probably doesn't go like this:

'You look so hot in that dress.'

'Shall we try Prada next?'

'Do you want to go get a latte?'

A lot of girls also nominate celebrity fashion icons as their role models. 'She's my role model, I love her style,' a girl might say of Leighton Meester or Blake Lively.

The twist is that the cashed-up celebrities decked out in designer labels rarely have to pay for them. They are showered with the stuff by fashion houses and sponsors who know it will translate into sales. Most of the profits made by the big labels come not from sales of high-end couture garments but from selling the dream to average girls and women willing to spend a bit extra on perfume or undies that bear the designer label.

I wouldn't say it is important to own designer labels, usually because nobody else really knows if it's designer or not – however, I am not going to lie, I love my designer labels. I feel the quality of the clothes is better and lots of designers have their own cool style . . .

I once saw lots of pictures of celebrities holding a type of phone and automatically really wanted one. It was nice, expensive and wasn't compatible with my cell phone network but since heaps of celebrities had it I thought it was cool. People who see something on a celebrity . . . suddenly think it is a thousand times better than if they saw it in a shop window . . . it is the person who is wearing or holding it that makes them want it.

Paris, 14

As much as 'it's what's on the inside that counts', I still feel it's nice to know you have the latest clothing, etc. – although I don't get upset if I'm not 'up with the latest fashion' because I like to be an individual.

Renee, 15

What mums and dads don't realise is that even though we are happy with ourselves, we as girls feel that if we don't have all the latest clothes we will not fit in and not be comfortable in our own skin.

Maddi, 16

What is a label worth?

'status anxiety' = anxiety about whether other people judge you as a success or a failure

I travel around the country and meet girls from all kinds of backgrounds. What I have found is that girls from more well-off homes tend to be the least interested in labels. In fact, some will prefer to look for cool op shop finds, to enhance the individuality of their look. That is because these girls are already perched at the top of the social ladder and have the least to prove.

The greatest pressure is felt by those who have the lowest disposable income. Ironically, it is girls who can least afford them that have the greatest social need to display prestige brands and products. For them, the right brands can feel especially important to their sense of worth.

By continually stressing that in order to *fit in* we need to *buy in* to their labels, companies are placing unfair stress on the least wealthy. Some teen girls feel as much status anxiety as their parents and are just as worried about having the right brands and maintaining their social status. The cure for this anxiety? According to advertisers and marketers, it would seem that the solution is to go shopping for yet more brand-label products.

If a girl is unable to afford the brands she has been told will make her desirable, sexy and 'worth it', what is she supposed to do? I have met countless teen girls who scrimp and save and do without all sorts of necessities just so they can buy a particular product.

Perhaps the longing for branded self-worth is also partly why we have seen an explosion in the market for designer knock-offs. Everyone wants to buy into the dream and this is the only way some people can. I don't feel too sorry for the huge corporations when they cry foul about fakes – after all, they created the consumer lust. It could be argued they have fallen victim to their own marketing campaigns.

More worrying is the fact that some girls and women are willing to do whatever it takes to get the designer labels they want. Theft is a tempting way to get otherwise unattainable luxury goods.

Using one's body as currency is another. To a certain degree, you have been primed to see that as socially acceptable. When a man showers a woman with expensive gifts, you may have seen other adults call him a catch and urge the lucky woman to snap him up. If she gets engaged to him, the first words she's likely to hear from other women are 'Let me see the rock!' – as if her worth as a person is measured in carats. These may seem like harmless examples, but I think we see their echoes in the very real and very disturbing instances of teenage girls giving in to sexual pressure from guys who promise them designer handbags or shoes.

Beyond the brand

Some of the intangible things you crave – a feeling of belonging, of admiration and acceptance, and of connection with others – are what designer labels and department stores are really promising to deliver, not just jackets and perfumes and iPods.

When we go shopping, are we really searching for a sense of belonging, a sense of community and a feeling of self-worth that we aren't finding in day-to-day life?

Are we building up our armour on the outside because we feel as though there isn't enough substance underneath?

The advertisers' and marketers' promises of a better life through products are just an illusion, of course. Like many girls, you may have had a trip to the local shopping centre for some retail 'therapy' and found that you arrived home feeling strangely . . . empty. That's your inner voice telling you that shopping can meet only some of your needs. For deeper feelings of connection and self-worth, we need to look for something more real, more lasting.

Most of the time, when we go shopping we set out in the belief that buying things will make us happier. There is evidence, though, that the pressure on us to buy more and more products can end up making us *less* happy. Just as Dorothy's friends in *The Wizard of Oz* discovered that the Wizard was all smoke and mirrors and they would have to look within themselves for the qualities they sought – intellect, emotions and courage – we need to look beyond advertising and marketing wizardry to find what will make us genuinely happy and whole.

Some researchers believe that corporations take advantage of the fact that many young people feel a void in their home life because parents are spending more and more time out of the house working (so they can afford to buy things for their family!). They say that it is easier for brands to capture the heart and mind of a teenager who doesn't get to spend much time with her parents, because she will be looking elsewhere for roots. It's no wonder then that girls I've spoken to say one of the things they like best about shopping trips with their mums is simply the chance to spend time together. Sixteen-year-old Steph speaks for a lot of girls when she says, 'I don't really go shopping with my mum all that often, about once a month, but when we do go shopping it's good because we both get to catch up on things.'

If connection with your parents is what you're really craving, then let them know it isn't always just their credit card you're after!

❧

A man is not a financial plan

Now more than ever, you need to know how to look after your money. This is because consumerism will no doubt be a feature of our culture for many years, if not generations, to come. The global credit crunch was also a stark reminder of the need for financial savvy. And due to the ageing of our population, when you reach retirement age, it is forecast that the government will be unable to afford a pension system on the same scale as today's.

Yet many teenagers are entering adult life not with an understanding of personal finance but with debt. Almost 10 per cent of people who went bankrupt in Australia in 2007 were only 15 to 24 years old. The same age group accounted for over 20 per cent of people who signed debt agreements, an alternative to declaring bankruptcy.

Many of the young people who are in debt report having a high level of stress about it. The highest stress level is among those who owe money to credit card companies: in the YouthSCAN survey in 2007, almost half of them said they were anxious about it.

Mobile phone bills run a close second when it comes to financial stress for teens. A spokeswoman for the New South Wales government's Office of Fair Trading said financial counselling services have 'young people in their late teens, early 20s, suggesting they should become a bankrupt because they have racked up thousands of dollars in premium services on mobile phones'. Fees for premium services – downloads, ringtones, voting on reality TV shows, competition entries – can snowball without you realising. The true cost is often buried in ambiguously worded print that seems to have been sized for ants to read.

What makes this especially unfair is that companies sell premium services by playing directly on the insecurities that many teen girls have. Flip to the back of *Dolly* or *Girlfriend* and you'll see ads for mobile phone wallpapers that are mostly variations of the 'Don't cha wish your girlfriend was hot like me?' theme. You can also download wallpaper featuring the picture of a hunk from *Home and Away*, or an anonymous young shirtless guy with ripped abs. There are ads for SMS chat services offering you the opportunity to chat and flirt with hundreds of guys. Then, when the pressure to be hot and sexy has got too overwhelming, you can consult an internationally renowned, guaranteed 99.9 per cent accurate love psychic via SMS, so that the future looks clearer.

Think of all the positive, cool things we could be using mobiles for. Yet this technology is being used to recycle tired old ideas of what a girl's future happiness should consist of: being hot and sexy, and getting a guy.

Another stubbornly persistent idea is that a girl doesn't need to worry about her financial future, because a knight in shining armour will one day come along with enough cash to pay off the mortgage and ensure a comfortable retirement. Despite all the advancements that have been made in gender equality, there are girls – and grown women – who do still hold on to this dream. Too many teenage girls tell me it doesn't matter what they want to be when they leave school, because they'll 'marry a rich man anyway'.

The truth is, there is no guarantee that will happen, so you need to grow up to be a financially independent woman.

I stress the importance of financial independence to all young women. As I say to my daughter, Lucy, a man is not a financial plan!
Elizabeth Broderick, Sex Discrimination Commissioner and Commissioner Responsible for Age Discrimination

I have made two saving accounts so that half of my pay goes into one and the other half into the other. One saving account is for me to use just for things such as going to the movies with friends or clothes or food, etc. The other account is locked so I cannot get any money out of it unless I go into the actual bank. The money in this account is my savings for the future.

My friend had set up two accounts and I thought it was a good idea so I asked my parents about it and they let me do it, too.
Steph, 16

I do save money for the future; I think it's very important so that you have some funds so if an emergency crops up it's there for you. My parents set it up for me when I was two years of age. Therefore I just grew up with it, was encouraged to save my whole life.

Renee, 15

Action plan

Maximise the mobile phone plan. One of the easiest ways to build up large debts is through your mobile phone. Many teen girls I know have managed to rack up bills of $400 or even over $500 on their mobiles in a month simply because they did not really understand the plan they were on. Sound familiar?

To keep your bills manageable, be clever about the plan you sign up for. My 13-year-old daughter's plan includes unlimited texting and unlimited social networking. It suits her perfectly because texting and using Facebook are the only things she really does on her phone. You may remember the story of the 13-year-old Californian girl who sent 14,528 text messages in one month, ending up with a bill 440 pages long. Her rate of text messaging – one SMS every two minutes during every waking hour – was totally over the top, but at least this girl's parents had her on the right plan, one that allowed unlimited texting! Using the mobile company's plan to your advantage – now, that is smart. Setting limits is smart, too. The girl's parents set a new rule: no texting after dinnertime.

Cut the credit card. There are parents who opt to co-sign so their teen can have a credit card. Sound tempting to start nagging for this? Getting a credit card at an early age can be a terrible burden, as it may be many years before you earn a high enough wage to dig yourself out of a debt hole. Instead of saving for the future, you may instead be paying off outfits long out of fashion and consigned to the back of the closet.

Save. Have you heard about the magic of compound interest? By keeping money in a savings account, you will earn interest – and then you will earn interest on that accrued interest. Yes, you will make money without lifting a finger. And if you put even a small amount from your allowance or wage into your savings account on a regular basis, the compound interest will pile up even faster.

Let's say you started saving just $10 per week from the beginning of high school. Six years later, when you finished high school, you would have $3,120 in savings alone. Now let's add your compound interest bonus of $506 (assuming your savings account had an interest rate of 5 per cent). You would have a total balance of $3,626 to spend at schoolies! Earning $506 for doing nothing other than saving seems a pretty sweet deal to me. If you haven't set up a savings account already, now is the time.

Learn to stop nagging. Companies know that one of the greatest selling tools at their disposal is the nag factor. Through ads and other marketing ploys they actively encourage you to nag – the marketers actually refer to this as 'pester power'. You may think (or know!) that if you ask often enough, eventually you will get what you want. Think Veruca Salt from *Charlie and the Chocolate Factory* ('I want it now, Daddy!').

Before nagging, weigh up how important this particular product really is to you. If you truly believe that it is something you need, put forward a good case explaining why. Here are some great ideas:

+ offer to pay part of the bill from your allowance or part-time wages;
+ set up a savings plan so you can work towards affording it yourself; or
+ ask to take on extra chores around the house until you have earned it.

I know these ideas might not sound as appealing as just holding your breath until your parents give in, but trust me, they will be grateful that you have grown out of nagging. And – trust me again – you will feel so much more proud of yourself and enjoy your purchase so much more if you have earnt it yourself.

> 'eclectic' = selected from a variety of sources

Try eclectic shopping. Next time you go out shopping, mix up the mall shopping with a trip to the local Vinnies or Lifeline to search for vintage finds. Hunting for treasures is fun, especially when you snag a really chic item. It's cheap. It's a way for you to put your own individual stamp on your look, an antidote to the dressed-entirely-in-recognisable-labels trend. And the vintage look gets the fashionista nod of approval.

Stand by your own individual style, too. You don't always have to get another person's say-so before you buy an item. If you really like it and want to wear it, just. Do. It.

Celebrate giving. We are not born materialistic; it is something we learn as we absorb messages from the culture around us. In fact, the pressure to keep up with everyone else's consumerist expectations can weigh heavily on a girl who doesn't want as many 'things' as other girls do or as adults expect her to. It can come to a head around big gift-giving times such as her birthday and Christmas.

I met a wonderful girl once who had actually been dreading her 14th birthday. There was the persistent question 'What do you want?' to which she drew a blank. She wasn't looking forward to a big birthday party and opening all the presents (that she felt she didn't need). Sensing her daughter's stress, her mum asked what would *really* make her happy on her birthday.

The girl decided that she didn't want her friends to bring her presents; she wanted them to bring presents *for dogs*. On her birthday, she happily tore open the beautifully wrapped dog toys and treats, and then she went with some of her friends to the local dog shelter and gave the dogs all the presents. She and her friends agree that it was their favourite birthday party ever.

A dog birthday party might not be exactly the right thing for you, but as this story shows, you can be creative in your approach to gift receiving – and giving.

Appreciate all that money can buy. I believe that girls have a strong sense of social justice and an urge to be socially responsible and nurturing of others. Just like the girl who wanted to help homeless dogs on her birthday, many girls are just waiting for the opportunity to share, to give.

I tell girls that wanting to make money is not bad, because with money you can help to change the world. Sometimes with groups of girls I work with, I demonstrate this by making a donation to World Vision in the girls' names. The money – less than $30 – provides immunisation to protect children in third-world countries from deadly diseases. I see a switch being turned on in these girls' minds when they realise that a relatively small amount of money, given in their own names, will actually save people's lives.

There are plenty of opportunities to get involved in helping others by making donations or doing volunteer work for causes that mean something to you.

Appreciate all that money cannot buy. As a much-needed reminder of the things in your life that are more valuable than any price tag can convey, you can try this exercise, inspired by a contest in which children were asked to submit a short essay or artwork on the topic 'What I really want that money can't buy'. The kids' answers were compelling, such as the winning essay:

> What I really want that money can't buy is unconditional love . . . My parents love me and buy me many things. But what tells me they love me the most is when they listen to me. Things are great, but what I really want is their time. What my friends really want is their parents' time. Maybe go for a walk, and talk. Maybe a bike ride and a lecture talk about money. If you

just do stuff together and smile, I will know you love me.

Erika C, 14

Try writing down your own answer. You may be surprised by what is revealed.

Affirmations

My own value is greater than any designer label.

I am free to develop my own sense of style.

6

Rage and Despair: Girls in Crisis

From time to time girls at our Enlighten Education events pull me aside to ask about friends they are worried about: 'Danni, I am just not sure whether I should tell her parents or not. I don't want to betray her trust but I don't know what else to say to help her.' When you love someone and they are in crisis, it hurts. Fact. And it is also a fact that there are times when we get caught up in self-destructive behaviours, too, and need to ask for help.

It is my hope that by talking about rage and despair openly and honestly, you will feel encouraged to reach out for yourself and for those you are worried about.

Why are girls in crisis?

While each girl's situation at home, school, with friends and in the community influences her life in a unique way, there are underlying factors in our culture that are putting more teenage girls at risk than ever before. Girls 'are in a crisis of rage and despair', says respected therapist and author Martha B. Straus. I believe that understanding and acknowledging this rage and despair are the first steps towards healing.

Being part of society means meeting certain expectations. Around adolescence girls begin to be more fully aware of the pressure to fulfil these expectations, which were mapped out before they were even born. Girls learn they will be rewarded with praise and acceptance if they fit into an ideal: they should be feminine girls, on the way to becoming feminine women.

In fact, a book written for teen girls I read offered this advice: 'Just think of all the wonderful things you get to experience as a girl. You get to wear gorgeous clothes, dresses and high heels, experiment with makeup and different hair styles ... just imagine if you were born a boy ... you'd never get to try on as many outfits as you'd like when shopping ... and you'd always be expected to change the flat tyre!' I happen to know the educator who wrote that particular book and she is a delightful woman and a dedicated teacher, but boy oh boy does that advice scare me. It is incredibly limiting – agree?

For teenage girls just beginning to become independent and to master their talents, the feminine ideal can seem frustratingly narrow: pretty, thin, attractive, friendly, agreeable, selfless, nurturing and soft-hearted. There is nothing wrong with these qualities. But a problem arises when adolescent girls feel pressured to act this way to the exclusion of other, more 'masculine' qualities in themselves, such as assertiveness, leadership, courage, physical strength, competitiveness, ambition and clear-headedness (and perhaps the desire to change tyres!).

Girls can hardly miss the messages from the people around them, school and popular culture about what it takes to be an ideal girl or the ideal woman. Unable to match the ideal no matter how they try, many girls begin to loathe themselves for falling short. Many women continue this self-loathing in their adult lives.

To try to meet the expectations of who they should be, teenage girls may have to tame themselves, blunt themselves. They learn that if they express anger, they will turn people off, because feminine, good girls are agreeable, not cranky. Swallowing anger can lead to confusing teen-girl behaviour. Even though on the surface you and your friends may appear sad, happy or indifferent, you may be bottling up rage. Where does girls' suppressed anger go? For some, it may gradually become depression. Girls may seek escape in drugs and alcohol. And for some, anger transforms into self-aggression: anorexia, bulimia, self-harm, suicide. Similarly, girls tend to be wary of fully displaying their intellect or admitting to other 'bad' emotions such as jealousy, guilt, loneliness, insecurity, sadness and anxiety.

Though adolescence is generally seen as a time of growth and development, there is also an aspect of loss during these years. You may grieve for the time when you were a little girl and feel a certain sadness that everything seems to be so much more complicated. My Program Manager for Enlighten in New Zealand, Rachel Hansen, told me about when she hit puberty:

> I was 12 and very reluctant to grow up – life was good as a little girl! On the day my period started I was playing make-believe games with my little brother and sister in our garden and I noticed blood on my undies. I cried and cried and cried. I sat by the window for the rest of the day, watching my siblings play, having decided with great sadness that now I had my period I was too old to play those games. I felt a real sense of loss, and also despair that I was no longer in control of my body.

In this chapter I want to explain some of the more common crises girls may experience during adolescence and offer you early warning signs so that you will know when to seek help for yourself or for the girls you care about.

Trigger warning: Pages 161 to 190 contain references to eating disorders, self-harm, depression, suicide and substance abuse that may be a trigger for some people.

'trigger warning' = a warning used most often in the media and online to alert people who may have a strong and potentially damaging response to certain subjects if they see, read or hear about them without warning

Eating disorders

In the eating disorder *anorexia nervosa*, a girl drastically reduces her food intake. In *bulimia nervosa*, she binges, eating excessive amounts of high-calorie foods, then soon after purges the food by vomiting. Feeling guilty and ashamed, she may not eat for several days after a binge.

Bulimia tends to be a more hidden condition because a bulimic may be close to an average weight, while in time an anorexic girl is likely to become visibly starved. One teen who has had bulimia nervosa for eight years told me, 'I'm at a normal weight now and if you saw me on the street, you wouldn't think I had an eating disorder at all.' Girls with anorexia or bulimia may maximise their weight loss by excessively exercising, or taking laxatives, diet pills or diuretics (which are normally used to reduce water retention).

Generally, a girl with anorexia or bulimia has a

distorted view of her own body. She is likely to think she is ugly. Even if she is dangerously thin, she may look in the mirror and see herself as very overweight. She may believe she is inherently worthless, a bad girl who deserves to be punished. Her waking hours revolve around food, her weight and her appearance, but she is unaware that her self-perceptions and harsh dietary rules are dysfunctional. Focusing on these things and exerting strict control over her body may be her way of dealing with difficult emotions or a sense of lack of control over other aspects of her life.

An eating disorder that gets less media attention than anorexia and bulimia is *binge-eating disorder*. A girl with this disorder will eat excessive amounts of food, often in secret, without purging afterwards. Underlying the condition there can be feelings of shame, guilt, self-loathing, depression and difficulty expressing feelings.

Welcome to the Wasteland

For those of us who have never had an eating disorder it can be hard to understand the grip that diseases such as anorexia and bulimia have on young women's minds. One of the most powerful descriptions of what it is like to live with these illnesses was sent to me by a 20-year-old woman whose anorexia and bulimia have brought her to the brink many times. It takes us right to the heart of what it means to have an eating disorder. I first met this talented young Sydney woman through my work with Enlighten, and I feel fortunate to have developed a genuine connection with her since. I want to share an edited excerpt of her story so you can gain a better understanding of how damaging and dangerous these illnesses truly are.

If you could read my mind you would know how we see ourselves. Pathetic. Stupid. Ugly. Disgusting. Worthless. Useless. Fat. Lazy. Gluttonous. I could go on.

Yet others, when asked, will describe us with words we never imagined to be synonymous with ourselves. Witty. Intelligent. Together. In control. Hard working. High achieving. Compassionate. Energetic. Creative. Enthusiastic. Happy.

Welcome to the wasteland of eating disorders – contradictory in almost every way, and the epitome of self loathing. It is a world where nothing makes sense. It's a place where frightened children fall into a mirror which shatters before they can escape. And where 'leave me alone' actually means 'please help me' . . .

Our community is unlike any other. We band together in mateship, each strongly denying our own illness, only to turn around and engage in exactly what we are most afraid of our friends doing. We accuse others of being irrational, frustrating and even psychotic – yet simultaneously we delude ourselves into believing that 'one more time won't hurt,' when we are in fact swiftly killing our spirits, and ourselves, and it's only by the grace of Someone who is watching over us – or sheer fortune – that we're still here today . . .

We dream of food, think of food, are obsessed with and possessed by food, and at the same time wave plates away with our hands and hold our breath walking past McDonald's. We eat carrot sticks in public, spending our nights eating everything in the pantry then acting out gut-wrenching, throat-shredding compensatory behaviours, which rip our bodies and minds apart. Or we've got the 'normal eating' in public down pat yet eat nothing but soy sauce and vegemite at home, or spit out our food when no one is watching . . .

We swing between believing we need help, not wanting help, denying we need help and not feeling as though we deserve help. And back . . . We end up close to dying, with all evidence before us, and repeatedly deny that we are so much as ill.

We say sorry over and over. Sorry for taking up so much space. Sorry for getting in your way. Sorry for voicing an opinion. Sorry for saying no. Sorry for saying yes. Sorry for thinking. Sorry for eating. Sorry for breathing. Sorry. Sorry. Sorry. Sorry. Sorry . . .

We acknowledge that we will have to work hard to achieve . . . recovery, but when the going gets tough we baulk. We begin once again to listen to the voice in our heads that convinces us that we're not sick, or, in times of negotiation, that we're simply 'not sick enough' . . .

We can remember every minute detail of our week's food intake and the calorie content of food we'd never so much as touch, and can recite our meal plans in our sleep. Yet sometimes we can't remember what day it is. We live in a world where intelligence is measured by how many people we can deceive, rather than what we achieve.

Welcome to the wasteland of anorexia and bulimia.

I've read this account many times. I cry every time I read it. Can you see, too, how serious eating disorders are? They are not something you should try to help a friend get through by yourself. They are not something you should struggle with alone. They are about so much more than just food.

Health effects of eating disorders

All eating disorders exact a terrible toll not only a girl's mental health, but on her physical health, too. Anorexia and bulimia affect all of the body's systems, from the skin, hair, teeth and nails through to all the body's tissues and internal organs, especially the heart and kidneys. Loss of menstrual periods and infertility can occur. In severe cases, death results from heart attack or organ failure. Binge-eating disorder carries with it health risks such as heart disease, stroke and diabetes.

Girls with anorexia or bulimia are often perfectionists and they may see asking for help to combat the disorder as a sign of moral weakness. A girl may cling to her eating disorder in the belief that it is the only way she can cope with the stresses of life. This means that telling a girl with an eating disorder to 'just snap out of it' will only make it seem to her that you don't understand. What she needs is caring help from professionals with experience in adolescent mental health and eating disorders.

There can be many facets to treatment. A girl may have regular sessions with a therapist. It may help her if the whole family also has therapy sessions together. Antidepressant or anti-anxiety medication may be prescribed by a specialist, and a GP and a nutritionist may be involved in treatment.

The suicide risk of a person who has an eating disorder is 37 times higher than average and it is not uncommon for sufferers to have other problems, such as depression, anxiety, substance abuse, the urge to self-harm or prior sexual abuse. For treatment to be truly successful, all such problems need to be addressed.

The dark side of dieting

As if round-the-clock exposure to media and advertising images of extremely thin models and celebrities isn't bad enough, there are also the 'pro-ana' and 'pro-mia' sites on the internet. These are sites where people with eating disorders who do not want to be treated share tips on how to lose more weight and evade treatment. Users post 'thinspiration' in the form of pictures of emaciated women and girls.

The effects of these sites can be devastating. One study showed that 96 per cent of adolescents with eating disorders who viewed pro-eating-disorder sites learned new techniques for losing weight and took longer to recover. Another study showed that these sites can also endanger people who do not have eating disorders. When a random sample of female university students were shown a pro-ana site, afterwards they had lower self-esteem, saw themselves as heavier than before, and became more preoccupied with exercise and weight loss.

Yet the biggest risk factor for developing an eating disorder is not exposure to shocking websites or images of dangerously thin celebrities. It is something that girls and women regularly encourage each other to try: frequent and extreme dieting. It is never a good idea to compete with your friends to reach the lowest weight.

'We often see groups of girls who will go on diets

together and when the other girls later resume normal eating patterns, one or two core girls will stay entrenched in this space,' says Dr Brent Waters, former professor of child and adolescent psychiatry at the University of New South Wales. How often have you heard a girl say, or in fact said yourself, 'I wish I could get anorexia, just for a couple of weeks'? It's always jokey in tone, but beneath it is a truth that other girls cannot fail to grasp.

We cannot completely block out the stream of thin-girl images flooding our lives. What we do have total control over is the example we set, the role model we provide. And that means being mindful of our words, adopting a healthy, balanced way of eating and learning to love our own bodies. Friends don't let friends fat talk. Agree?

Early intervention is key to treating an eating disorder, and this means first recognising that starvation dieting is not a natural part of being a teenage girl. Eating disorders have become so commonplace that there is almost an expectation that a girl will show signs of one at some point. Dr Waters says, 'There is an old viewpoint that adolescence is just a difficult stage, yet the evidence shows quite the opposite: it need not be. Eating disorders, self-harm – all signify real problems of one sort or another that are driving the behaviour. They are not merely rites of passage.'

Eating disorder warning signs

* Extreme dieting, such as cutting out entire food groups or skipping meals
* Overeating
* Weight loss or gain
* Obsession with appearance or weight
* Loss of menstrual periods or disrupted menstrual cycle
* Sensitivity to the cold
* Faintness, dizziness, fatigue
* Anxiety, depression, irritability or an increase in mood swings
* Withdrawing from friends and family
* An increased interest in preparing food for other people
* Food rituals such as eating certain foods on certain days
* Wearing baggier clothes
* Exercising to an excessive degree
* Frequent excuses for not eating
* Eating slowly, rearranging food on the plate or using other strategies to eat less, such as eating with a teaspoon
* Eating quickly
* Stockpiling food in the bedroom
* Food disappearing from the pantry
* Frequent trips to the bathroom after meals

Self-harm

Self-harm is when a girl purposely injures herself, usually in secret. There are many different ways that a girl might do this, including:

+ cutting, burning, biting or branding her skin;
+ hitting herself or banging her head;
+ pulling her hair out;
+ picking and pulling at her skin; or
+ picking at old sores to open them up again.

In some cases it is a form of risk-tasking and rebelling, or even of being accepted into a peer group. In others, it is a sign of deep psychological distress, a way of coping with painful, overwhelming feelings. If a girl finds it hard to express emotions such as anger, sadness or grief, marking her body in this way may be her desperate attempt at self-expression. A girl numbed by depression or trauma may self-harm in order to feel something again.

It can also be a cry for help. A girl who doesn't know whom to ask for help, or how, may be using her injured body to send a message. And as with eating disorders, there are girls who self-harm because they feel that they are not in control of aspects of their life. For them, self-harm is a way of asserting control.

During the act of hurting herself, a girl may feel as though she is releasing pent-up steam, as if opening the valve on a pressure cooker. The act brings a temporary sense of relief. But self-harm also brings with it guilt, depression, self-loathing, anger, fear and isolation from friends and family.

Self-harm doesn't necessarily mean that a girl is suicidal, but all cases of self-harm need to be taken seriously. Self-harm can be related to mental health issues including depression, psychosis, bipolar disorder and borderline personality disorder. It can also be due to a trauma, such as physical or sexual abuse, or to some other source of deep psychological pain.

Self-harm may do lasting physical damage. While girls rarely need hospitalisation because of self-harm, they may give themselves lifelong scarring as well as nerve damage.

A girl who self-harms needs to learn other ways to cope when the urge strikes. A therapist is likely to suggest ideas such as counting to ten or waiting 15 minutes, to give the feeling a chance to pass. They may suggest saying out loud 'No!' or 'Stop!' Relaxation techniques such as yoga or going for a run or doing some other kind of hard physical exercise can also help.

Don't be alarmed if some of the advice you or a friend receives sounds a little unconventional. For instance, if the urge to self-harm is unbearable to resist, one of the suggested solutions is for a girl to choose an alternative, such as squeezing ice cubes between her fingers until they go numb, eating a chilli, standing under a cold shower, having her legs waxed or drawing in red on her body instead of cutting.

Crucially, the underlying reasons why a girl self-harms need to be uncovered and worked through with a professional, who will also help her to develop healthier ways of identifying, coping with and expressing painful emotions.

Self-harm warning signs

- Cuts – especially small shallow parallel cuts on the arms or legs – for which there is no adequate explanation
- Other frequent and unexplained injuries, such as burns or bruises
- Starting to wear long sleeves or pants all the time, even in warm weather
- Sudden aversion to going swimming or getting changed in front of other girls
- Hair missing, where it has been deliberately pulled out
- Mood changes, depression, anxiety
- Spending a lot of time alone
- Notable difficulty dealing with stressful or emotional situations
- A drop in school performance

Depression

Right now, between 2 and 5 per cent of young Australians are suffering from depression. By the time they are adults, around one in five of them will have experienced it. Unfortunately, some of these young people will go through adolescence without their depression being recognised or treated. As adults tend to expect that the teenage years will be a turbulent time of extreme emotions, sometimes teen depression slips under the radar.

Depression is not the same as having a blue day now and then, feeling a bit down sometimes or being sad for a brief time in response to a disappointment or loss. These things are a normal part of life for an adolescent – and for an adult.

Depression is a clinical condition involving a disturbance in brain chemistry that causes a change in mood: from a state of balance to one of sadness or irritability. Depression decreases the brain's ability to feel joy and pleasure. For instance, a depressed girl may suddenly stop playing netball or going shopping with her friends. The chemical changes in the brain also affect other body systems and behaviour: a depressed girl's appetite may increase or decrease; she may sleep more or less than usual; she may find it hard to concentrate; and she may feel tired and lacking in energy.

The causes of depression are multilayered and differ from one individual to another. A girl can inherit a predisposition to develop depression. It can be triggered by a stressful event, such as the death of a loved one or the divorce of her parents. And personality may play a role, with anxious, self-critical and sensitive people being at greater risk, according to the Black Dog Institute.

It can be tricky to identify depression in teens because they may have real difficulty identifying and explaining how they are feeling. Teens are undergoing so many other developmental changes at the same time that adults may also be uncertain whether the changes in their mood and behaviour are simply a normal part of growing up. And rather than a sad mood, the only indication that a girl has depression may be that she starts behaving differently. For instance, she might start to do worse in school or want to spend more time alone. She might start doing new risky things, such as driving recklessly, being promiscuous, taking drugs or drinking alcohol.

You know your friends best, so trust your gut instincts. If you feel that for a period of two weeks or more one of your friends has not been the girl you recognise, seek advice from a trusted adult. Same goes for you, too.

It is important to treat teen depression as these are important years when a girl undergoes changes that will be crucial to her happiness later in life. This is when you and your friends are becoming independent, developing learning skills, forming your sexual identity, creating relationships and preparing for your future careers. Having depression can interfere with all of these. Depression also places a girl at greater risk of substance abuse, self-harm and eating disorders. At its most severe, depression can cause a girl to try to take her life.

Treating depression

An antidepressant medication may become part of a girl's treatment plan. The doctor is likely to start her on a low dose and raise the dosage gradually over a week or two. It can be up to eight weeks before the drug begins to have its full effect. Not all antidepressants work on all patients in exactly the same way, so the doctor may recommend swapping to a different type of medication or making further changes to the dosage.

With many antidepressants, if a girl suddenly takes herself off the drug – goes 'cold turkey' – it can result in some frightening side effects such as anxiety, insomnia, nausea, and pins and needles. It is vital to follow the instructions when taking an antidepressant and to consult a doctor before coming off it.

It is also important that the doctor knows what else a girl is taking. For instance, taking certain antidepressants with the herbal supplement St John's Wort can result in a dangerous interaction. The same goes with illegal drugs.

Psychological treatment is also important. One common and successful type is cognitive behavioural therapy

(CBT), which can be done one-on-one with a therapist or in a small group. The aim of CBT is to reveal the ways in which thought patterns affect mood, and to teach a girl how to challenge her negative thoughts and beliefs. Other types of counselling or therapy may focus on aspects of a girl's personality or events in the past that may have put her at risk of depression.

Depression warning signs

+ Uncharacteristic risk-taking such as driving recklessly, being promiscuous, taking drugs or drinking alcohol
+ Sadness
+ Irritability
+ Mood that varies throughout the day, especially feeling worse in the morning and better as the day progresses
+ Less interest in doing things she used to enjoy
+ Increase or decrease in appetite
+ Sleeping more or less than usual
+ Restlessness
+ Tiredness, fatigue
+ A drop in school performance, due to decreased concentration
+ Wanting to spend more time alone
+ Expressing feelings of guilt, worthlessness or hopelessness

+ Increased sensitivity to pain, and new aches and pains
+ Apathy and lack of motivation
+ Dwelling on death or suicide

❦

Suicide

It may come as a surprise that in females, the highest-risk time for suicide is not the teenage years. The highest rate of suicide in females occurs in the age group that many teen girls' mums belong to: women aged between 35 and 44. In fact, teen girls have the lowest rate of suicide of all females. That statistic is little comfort, of course. Just one teen suicide is too many. Just one adult suicide is too many. The reason that knowing the statistics is helpful is that they remind us to be mindful of not only our emotional health but also our parents', too.

Many people who try to take their lives share a sense of being trapped in a stressful or painful situation, a situation that they are powerless to change. Having depression or a mental illness raises a person's risk of suicide. Stressful life events or ongoing stressful situations may fuel feelings of desperation or depression that can lead to suicide attempts. Examples of these stresses include the death of a loved one, divorce or a relationship break-up, a child custody dispute, settling in to a blended family, financial trouble, or a serious illness or accident.

Any kind of abuse – physical, verbal or sexual – increases the risk. That applies not only to teens but their mothers and fathers as well, even if that abuse took place many years ago yet is unresolved. Substance abuse by any member of a family affects the other members of the family and can either directly lead to suicidal feelings or indirectly, through the loss of income and social networks or trouble with the law.

Looking at teens in particular, bullying needs to be taken seriously as it has been known to make children try to take their own lives. Also, teens are right in the middle of forming their own individual identities and a major component of that is their sexuality. For a teenager who is questioning their sexual preference or gender, the pressure to be like everyone else, the taunting they receive because they clearly are not, or their own guilt and confusion can become unbearable.

A relationship break-up can be a trigger for suicide in some teens. Adults have had time to learn to look at the bigger picture. They know that in years to come, a teenage break-up will not seem anywhere near as important as it does at the time.

I can look back now and see that after my first serious boyfriend broke up with me, I became very depressed and suicidal. It was more than just feeling sad. It was a huge blackness. A deep sense of being lonely. Unlovable. And to make things worse, whenever I tried to talk to my parents or teachers about how I was feeling, they would all just say that I would get over it and it was a normal part of life to feel heartbroken. They were right but they failed to see I needed help putting it all in perspective. And you know what? That pain was real. Yes, I did get over it and I have had great loves since, but that first experience of loss hurt the most. It was all so raw and confusing!

'taboo' = forbidden

Another trigger for teen suicide is the recent suicide of someone close to them, or the anniversary of a suicide or death of someone close to them. These are times when you, or your friends, may need extra support.

Suicide is hard to talk about. It is almost taboo, simply too painful to touch on. But silence can be deadly. Often people close to a teen girl at risk of suicide do not ask her the tough question of whether she is planning to take her own life. In part they may be in a state of denial, which is only human – after all, no one wants to imagine that a girl feels suicidal.

In fact, once when I mentioned I was feeling suicidal to a teacher, she told me to 'stop being silly and dramatic!'. I think this teacher was frightened that if she spoke to me about it, somehow she would be putting me at greater risk. Denial can seem easier, can't it? However, experts in adolescent mental health agree that it is more than okay to speak directly about suicide. 'I have never known a child to suicide because someone asked whether they were thinking about it,' says Dr Brent Waters. 'They should ask; the issues won't just go away.'

Another unhelpful myth about suicide is that a teen who talks about suicide is simply seeking attention and won't actually take her life. In fact, four out of five young people who commit suicide tell someone of their intentions beforehand. Besides, I have never understood the point of making a distinction between attention seeking, a cry for help or a genuine intention to commit suicide. Even if a girl is not actually going to go through with a plan to take her life, if she is distressed enough to cry out for help, her voice needs to be heard and she needs support.

Suicide warning signs

+ Loss of interest in activities she used to enjoy
+ Giving away her prized possessions
+ Thoroughly cleaning her room and throwing out important things
+ Violent or rebellious behaviour
+ Running away from home
+ Substance abuse
+ Taking no interest in her clothes or appearance
+ A sudden, marked personality change
+ Withdrawal from friends, family and her usual activities
+ A seeming increase in her accident proneness, or signs of self-harm

+ A change in eating and sleeping patterns
+ A drop in school performance, due to decreased concentration and feelings of boredom
+ Frequent complaints about stomach aches, headaches, tiredness and other symptoms that may be linked to emotional upsets
+ Rejection of praise or rewards
+ Verbal hints such as 'Nothing matters anyway'
+ Suddenly becoming cheerful after a period of being down, which may indicate she has made a resolution to take her life

What you can do

Reading the list of suicide warning signs is enough to freak out anyone, but there is much you can do to help someone who is suicidal. Number one: if anyone – child, adolescent or adult – says something like 'I want to kill myself' or 'I'm going to kill myself', seek help straightaway. Remove anything they might be tempted to use to kill themselves with and stay with them. Dial 000 if you need to, or a crisis line. The following phone counselling services are available throughout Australia 24 hours a day:

+ Lifeline: 13 11 14
+ Kids Help Line: 1800 55 1800
+ Salvation Army 24-hour Care Line: 1300 36 36 22

Another valuable thing you can do to help someone you fear is having suicidal thoughts is to listen. These pointers are adapted from the Victorian Government's excellent 'Youth suicide prevention – the warning signs' on www.betterhealth.vic.gov.au:

+ Listen and encourage her to talk
+ Tell her you care
+ Acknowledge her feelings
+ Reassure her
+ Gently point out the consequences of her suicide, for her and the people she leaves behind
+ Stay calm
+ Try not to panic or get angry
+ Try not to interrupt her
+ Try not to judge her
+ Don't overwhelm her with too much advice or stories about your own experiences

❧

Substance abuse

The greatest fear of many of the parents I meet through my work is that their teenage daughter will be exposed to drugs. I think the reason we parents are so concerned about drugs is that compared to when we were teens there are many different types of drugs, they're more widely available and some of the newer drugs are highly toxic and have unpredictable effects. It's no wonder adults feel a little panicky sometimes.

Panic can be a paralysing thing. Knowledge, however, is empowering. Parents' greatest fears often focus on harder drugs such as heroin, cocaine, ecstasy and crystal meth (ice), but these are in fact the drugs that teens are least likely to be exposed to. Heroin, cocaine and ecstasy are used by fewer than three teenagers in every hundred. Amphetamines, such as speed and crystal meth, are used by four in every hundred. On the other hand, 25 in every hundred teens have gotten high by inhaling spray paint, petrol, glue or solvent fumes. This practice is damaging to vital organs, including the brain.

That their teen will die from overdosing on hard drugs is one of most parents' greatest fears. Death from substance abuse at any age is tragic, but when a person dies so young, they lose so many years of life. And the emotional cost on their family and friends is huge. But to put the risk in perspective, drugs account for 6 per cent of deaths each year in people aged 15 to 24.

Make no mistake, hard drugs devastate or end the lives of the teens who use them. But don't fall into the trap of believing that the less headline-grabbing substances that larger numbers of teens are abusing are any less harmful. It turns out that two of the substances teens widely abuse are also the most widely abused by adults: alcohol and tobacco. The other is one that plenty of adults have used and that some even mistakenly believe is quite harmless: marijuana. Perhaps the reason teen abuse of alcohol, tobacco and marijuana doesn't cause as much alarm is that so many adults have also used or are currently using them.

I've already talked about all the damage alcohol can do. Tobacco causes cancer, heart disease, stroke, birth defects if a mother smokes while pregnant and respiratory diseases such as emphysema. Marijuana causes anxiety and panic attacks, raises the risk of heart attack, raises the risk of schizophrenia in certain people and causes problems with memory, learning and problem solving. It also contains cancer-causing chemicals.

Speaking more generally, substance abuse can cause:

+ damage to the heart, kidneys, liver and brain
+ blood-borne diseases such as hepatitis B and C, and HIV
+ accidents
+ psychosis
+ depression
+ brain damage
+ coma or death

Not only can some drugs contribute to brain damage, they can in fact change the way the brain works. This is of special concern for you and your friends, because in the teen years, the different parts of the brain are developing at different rates. In teens, the part of the brain that is geared towards avoiding risks hasn't caught up yet to the reward or pleasure centre of the brain.

'We know that adolescent brains are driven by reward, and younger people often do not have the brain maturity to put the brakes on things,' says Associate Professor Michael Baigent, senior consultant psychiatrist at Flinders Medical Centre.

This brain difference makes teens more vulnerable to substance abuse than adults. A strong urge to fit in with friends, plus the stresses that sometimes come with adolescence, also put teens at greater risk.

If most drugs are taken regularly enough, a person's tolerance increases and so a girl using drugs will need increasing dosages to get an effect. As she becomes more dependent, without the drug she suffers withdrawal symptoms. These can range from anxiety, depression, sleeplessness and racing heartbeat right through to difficulty breathing, shaking, vomiting, diarrhoea, seizure, hallucinations, heart attack and stroke.

Often a drug problem is one problem among others such as depression or an eating disorder, and these need to be treated as well. Treatment may include counselling, family therapy, CBT and meetings of groups such as Alcoholics Anonymous or Narcotics Anonymous. Medication sometimes is prescribed as treatment for conditions such as depression or anxiety. It may also be prescribed to ease withdrawal symptoms, suppress drug cravings or block the effects of a drug so it becomes pointless to take it.

If you or a friend have a substance abuse problem, talk to a trusted adult about it and ask for an appointment with a GP or community health centre for referral to a substance-abuse counsellor.

Substance abuse warning signs

+ Mood swings
+ Depression
+ Confusion
+ Agitation and irritability
+ Missing school or skipping classes
+ A drop in school performance
+ Getting into fights
+ Starting arguments or breaking rules more often
+ Changes in taste in music, hair or clothing, to a more unconventional style
+ Withdrawal from the family
+ Hanging out with a new, possibly older, crowd
+ A significant weight gain or loss
+ Red or glassy eyes
+ Extreme fatigue
+ Poor health

Prevention and intervention

I believe that no matter how troubled a girl is, she can turn her life around. The key is communication.

Many teen girls have a limited vocabulary for expressing their feelings, but you can help your friends to get problems off their chest. It can take something as simple as saying 'I feel really angry about this – do you?' to open the floodgates.

If you are bottling up feelings, find a trusted friend or adult in your life that you can talk to. And don't forget, there are free, 24-hour crisis lines that can help – see the 'Resources' section at the back of the book for numbers.

Feel free to express all your emotions, rather than choking on your darker feelings until they turn into despair. Encourage your friends to do the same. You deserve to feel such powerful feelings. As Martha Straus says, 'there is someone in there worth being mad about.'

Action Plan

Seek professional help. If you feel that you, or a friend, is showing warning signs of risky behaviour or a mood disorder, a good starting point is to talk to a trusted adult – a parent, school counsellor, favourite teacher, sports coach.

The next step may be to see a GP, for a referral to a relevant specialist, local adolescent mental health team, counsellor or community health centre. Medicare rebates are available for referrals to psychiatrists, clinical psychologists and social workers.

For an older teen especially, it may be easier said than done to get her to seek professional help. If your friend does not accept treatment, try to keep the lines of communication open. Let her know that you are there to offer support and help her get treatment if she changes her mind.

Banish secrecy. When we are in the midst of a crisis, a common reflex is to try to keep it secret from the outside world. A suicide attempt, an eating disorder, financial problems – whatever the crisis is, the tendency is to try and contain it within our own four walls. We do this out of embarrassment or an instinct to protect ourselves, or our friends, from judgement, pity or bullying.

Maintaining a shroud of secrecy around a crisis is not helpful, though. 'Secrets can be a dark thing within teen girl networks and a source of power for the holder of the secret,' according to Dr Waters.

Whenever a girl says she wants to tell me something and asks if I will keep it secret, I explain, 'I can keep secrets but if what you tell me involves you harming yourself, or anyone else hurting you in any way, then I am going to care about you enough to get you help. You can trust me – you can trust me to get you the help you need.' I have never had a girl decide not to tell me her pain after hearing this. In fact, I find girls actually feel comforted by knowing I am going to take the secret out of their hands and act for them. Try this approach next time a friend asks you to keep a dark secret.

Build networks of support. For teen girls, life is all about networks, isn't it? The best way to prevent problems, or support your friends on the road to recovery, is to forge strong, healthy networks. Networks may include doctors, therapists, adult mentors, other relatives, school counsellors, and friends at school and out of school. Find out what support networks you can access in your school and community.

Give a Book of Love. This is an idea that I was told about by a teen with an eating disorder. When I asked her to tell me the most healing thing someone had done for her, she said that it was when a friend sent her a Book of Love. 'It was just before I went into the most intensive treatment I've ever been in and I received a package in the mail,' she recalled. 'She'd filled a book with song lyrics, things she likes about me, inspiring quotes, and pretty stickers and other glittery things . . . She hadn't told me she was going to send it, and it was such a lovely surprise. She left the last ten pages blank for me to fill in with positive things about myself.' As with many people who have an eating disorder, this girl is also dealing with other issues: depression, anxiety, and a past history of suicide attempts and self-harm. I think the Book of Love is relevant for girls dealing with all such issues, to remind them how much they are cherished.

Celebrate. When you, or your friend, is on the path to recovery there may be frustrating and disappointing setbacks, but there will be victories, too. Take heart in them. And celebrate.

Affirmations
I listen with love, respect and an open heart.
I ask for help when I need it.

7

Schooling for Life

Confession. I loved school. Truly I did. In primary school, I was one of those kids who liked to sit right up the front – dead centre – so the teachers could see me at all times. I was desperate for their attention: 'Notice me! Love me! Be stunned by my brilliance!' By the time I was in high school, I usually sat up the back so I could also be noticed by my friends and engage in some sneaky girl-chatter between activities – but I still yearned to be praised by my teachers.

I even loved the smell of my teachers. My favourite teacher smelt like roses. I loved the smell of the stencils my teachers would hand out, too – they smelt like methylated spirits and if you took a good whiff when they were literally hot off the press, you could get a pleasant little head spin. A learning-high of sorts, a heady mix of fumes and ideas.

Stencils that smell like chemicals might sound incredibly old-fashioned to you with your fancy-pantsy 'SMART Boards' and 'online learning communities' (*Danni rolls her eyes at kids nowdays*).

But regardless how much technology advances, the core of a successful high school education has always been the development of lifelong learning skills. These learning skills are what will help you (as they helped me) in your tertiary studies, careers and adult life in general. What really matters is not whether you're learning by listening to a podcast or by writing down notes from a lecture. What matters are the fundamental skills you're developing for the future, such as the ability to learn new things, how to communicate with others and work in a team, planning and organisation, problem-solving, self-management and initiative.

It is especially important for you to master these core skills because the world is rapidly changing. And guess what? It is impossible for the educators who set high school curriculums to know for certain what content students will need to know in the future. Even seemingly modern teaching techniques such as the use of podcasts will seem old-fashioned in a few years' time. Schools are realising that they need to keep pace with change. They are focusing on helping students become lifelong learners who can adapt to changes in the world and in the workplace. Greg Whitby, who is the Executive Director of Catholic Schools for Western Sydney, writes:

> [T]hose who work in and for schools will have to work differently if they are to serve their students and society in the knowledge age of the 21st century ... We stand together at the beginning of a transformation of schooling for life.

Yep. You girls live and learn in exciting times.

It was probably inevitable that someone like me, who loved school so much, would become a teacher. Back when I was in a classroom, I taught English and history. Because there was often so much content to get through during class time, I rarely had the opportunity to really explain the learning process or help my students make sense of the things about school that worried them the most – such as how to manage their time and get all their homework done in time to watch *Beverly Hills 90210*.

(Disclaimer: I understand that many less-than-scholastic things worry you, too. My favourite Year 12 English class once gave me an award at their formal for being the teacher who helped them to 'understand and love Shakespeare, as well as figure out how to apply fake tan without getting streaks on our skin'. Danni = All. The. Big. Issues. For now, though, we shall focus on learning rather than avoiding Oompa Loompa–like skin.)

Sit back – or front and centre if that's what rocks your world – and let's spend some time examining why school really is incredibly relevant.

Learning like a girl

Learning styles tend to differ between girls and boys. This may partly be due to the difference in the ways that girls and boys are nurtured, but there are also differences in brain development and cognitive (thinking) development between boys and girls. According to the experts – and my years of experience in classrooms back this up – girls tend to have better language skills than boys of the same age. Girls usually talk more, have a wider vocabulary, and are more comfortable discussing and writing about their emotions.

Connections are important to teen girls in every part of life, including education. This means you tend to be more interested in studying with your peers. Girls are also able to concentrate for longer periods than boys. While boys often take an interest in technical details and processes, girls tend to be more engaged when they can see a practical application and usefulness to what they're learning. Research shows that it may not be maths, science and computing that many girls struggle with, but the way in which they are taught. If real-world examples are given and girls have the opportunity to apply their new knowledge, they may be better able to connect with those subjects. Do you agree?

These are general guidelines that may help you understand broadly how you learn. With these as a foundation, you can seek more opportunities to learn in ways that work for you, such as group study, discussion groups and practical application of knowledge. You can minimise types of learning that are less helpful, such as studying alone all the time or trying to memorise technical details without context.

There are exceptions to every rule, though. Each individual, whether girl or boy, is unique. People are influenced by more than just their gender, so you may differ in some respects from other girls. These differences can be beneficial. For instance, a girl might be switched on by learning about processes in a theoretical way as well as having better language skills than boys her age. Differences can also be frustrating. Think of a girl whose language skills are not quite as developed as those of the other girls in her year at school, when there is an assumption that English should come relatively easily to her.

The better you understand your individual learning

preferences, the better you can utilise suitable studying techniques and get additional help if you need it.

Think about your studying habits and ask yourself: 'How do I like to learn?' 'When, how and with whom do I do my best learning?' If you are unsure, ask your teachers. Find out what works and how you can make your learning environment at home even better.

❦

Log on

The three Rs – reading, 'riting and 'rithmetic – were once considered the basics of learning. And do you know what? Girls are shining in the more traditional subjects. In fact, girls outperformed boys by nearly two to one when it came to topping subjects in the 2010 New South Wales Higher School Certificate exams. Seventy girls achieved first place in at least one subject, compared with 37 boys. Nice work, Amazons!

But new technology means that the three Rs are now just a few of the tools a girl needs in her schoolbag. To make use of all the learning opportunities that will come your way in the future, you also need to be competent in a wide range of information and communications technology (ICT). Yet while girls are, on average, more successful at reading and writing than boys, evidence shows that girls are in trouble when it comes to ICT.

Many of you are just not embracing the cyber world to the same degree as boys.

In Australia, girls are more likely than boys to see ICT as boring (36 per cent of girls compared to 16 per cent of boys) or difficult (23 per cent to 11 per cent). The result is that more boys than girls study technology-related subjects. Out of all the students who took computer programming in the 2002 Higher School Certificate in New South Wales, fewer than one in five was female. The same trend was seen in TAFE enrolments. Girls and young women are at risk of becoming the information-poor and of being excluded from emerging technology jobs and fields of study.

To help address this imbalance, girls need to play to their strengths. Rather than trying to find ways to use computers in the same ways boys do, find new, creative ways to use them.

If you are one of the girls who are less interested than boys in learning computer programming and software design, perhaps it is because you don't consider this knowledge relevant to you. Girls tend to like connecting and communicating, and learn best when they can see the practical application of knowledge. Well, computer literacy is crucial to creating the kind of websites that offer you a chance to communicate and connect, such as Facebook, blogs and role-playing sites. True? Perhaps seeing this link will bring computing subjects to life for you.

THE GIRL WITH THE BUTTERFLY TATTOO

> 'patronise' = treat someone as though you are looking down on them

Researchers have suggested that another reason girls may lack interest in computing is that there are few positive female role models for girls within ICT. Did you ever see the infographic that went viral that posed the question 'Which Female Tech Influencer Are You?' By answering silly questions such as 'Jimmy Choos or running shoes?' and 'What's your must-have bag?' you are supposed to find out which successful female tech influencer you most resemble.

Please. I know this is just meant to be fun but really – isn't it incredibly patronising to suggest the biggest decision made by dynamos such as Google vice president Marissa Mayer and Facebook chief operating officer Sheryl Sandberg is which handbag they might like to take to work?

When you think of all the legends in the development of ICT, you rarely hear the names of women. The usual names that spring to mind are Steve Jobs, Bill Gates and Mark Zuckerberg. Can you imagine anyone asking Bill Gates how he prefers to style his hair?

Let's start celebrating the role of women in ICT, too. I am talking about women such as Ada Lovelace, who just happens to have been the first computer programmer in history. She wrote the first algorithm specifically for the computer. Then there is Grace Hopper, the inventor of the first computer language composed of words. And who were the original programmers of the first general-purpose computer?

> 'algorithm' = a step-by-step procedure in maths or computing for working out a calculation

Six women: Betty Holberton, Kay McNulty, Marlyn Wescoff, Ruth Lichterman, Betty Jean Jennings and Fran Bilas. Seek out your own female ICT *she*roes (see what I did right there?) and get amongst the techies and cyber geeks.

Get practical

If understanding the practical application of knowledge is your learning 'on' switch, you can use it to help you develop skills in any field, not just ICT. This was brought home to me when I was running The Lighthouse Project, a mentoring program for young people at risk of leaving school early. One of the volunteer mentors, a dedicated man named Glenn, was an officer in the RAAF. He was mentoring Rachel, a 14-year-old girl who found school irrelevant and boring. She had developed a sense of despair about her schooling.

Even though she didn't like science and maths at school, Glenn got her working in a highly technical arena where there could be no margin of error: a division known as Air Movements at the RAAF base in Richmond, New South Wales. This is the team that calculates safe loads for aircraft used in airlifts, such as the C-130, B707 and Caribou.

'Later, when we debriefed, Rachel recalled how boring it was poring over numbers, shapes, weights and dangerous cargo types,' says Glenn. Yet he couldn't help but notice that she was very taken with a good-looking pilot she had met. 'Then it dawned on me,' he says. 'I asked Rachel what all the science and maths she was continually complaining about, and couldn't understand, was useful for. The normal "Nothing" reply followed. I explained that the good-looking pilot's life was partly in her hands. I explained that the aircraft was like a seesaw. It needed to be perfectly balanced.' To avoid dangerous chemical reactions, he explained to Rachel, some types of cargo needed to be separated from others, by varying distances.

'And if it wasn't, I told her, the good-looking pilot's flight would be his last, and it would be the last of everybody else on board... To watch Rachel's face was like watching fireworks light up the night sky... She immediately grabbed the tables we use to calculate the necessary ratios and began asking intelligent, urgent questions so that she could help figure out the equations we needed to get the weight and balance ratio correct.'

Glenn was observant enough to find what it was that would turn the key so that Rachel, once unlikely to finish school let alone be into science and maths, was suddenly passionately interested. For each girl there is something that will make learning relevant. Find out what switches learning on for you and capitalise on that at every opportunity.

Keep your eye on the prize

One of the stubborn stereotypes about girls is that they lack the competitive spirit seen in boys. Too many people still believe that it is only boys, fuelled by testosterone and bravado, who are motivated by competition, who strive because they want to be victorious on the sporting field or in the classroom. This is absolute nonsense. Certainly I was a very competitive girl. At school, I wanted to be top of the class. At my part-time job at McDonald's, I thrived on being the fastest girl on the register.

'Girls *love* competition and rewards,' says Acting Head of Student Welfare at Sydney's Fairfield High School, Lisa Porter. 'In addition to the usual stickers, stamps and merits, I have a huge bag of prizes from a languages education supply company. The girls generally aim to collect the whole set: ruler, pencil, sharpener, eraser, badge and bookmark. Tangible recognition for their efforts is ... something to which they aspire.'

Get to know what motivates you the most. Is it going on special outings with friends? If so, tell yourself that you will not go to the next one until your assignment is finished. Is it seeing that you get the marks you know you deserve? If so, draw up a chart and hang it on your bedroom wall. In one column, write down assessment tasks that you have handed in. Next to each task, record the mark you realistically think you deserve for it. This should be possible to estimate as most teachers will give you their marking criteria when they hand out an assessment task. Then next to that, record the actual mark you receive when the teacher hands the task back to you.

Don't be afraid to make mistakes

We are in the midst of an overprotective parenting trend known as 'cotton-wool' or 'parachute' parenting, in which we adults try to protect you from every conceivable danger and conflict. This ranges from banning kids from walking anywhere in case they are bullied, hit by a car or targeted by a paedophile, through to parents intervening in even the most minor problems their children have at school or with friends.

The urge to protect our children is a natural one. But this instinct is greater now than ever before because your generation is the first to grow up with mobile phones, allowing parents and kids to check in with one another 24/7. We want to monitor our kids more often because, with continuous media exposure, we are all too aware of the accidents and crimes that can happen. And on average, we are having fewer children, later in life, and more often with the help of fertility treatments. Children have always been – and should always be – precious to their

'resilience' = the power to bounce back from setbacks in life

parents. It's just that never before have there seemed to be so many reasons to protect kids; nor have there ever been so many ways to monitor and protect them.

Even though our intentions are good, when we over-protect you we are actually taking away a much-needed learning opportunity: the opportunity for you to learn from your mistakes. The result of too much adult interven-tion is that you may have difficulty perceiving real danger, solving problems and resolving conflicts with others.

Consultant psychologist Dr Judith Paphazy, who has worked with students, teachers and parents in Australian schools, believes that 'children are becoming less resil-ient and self-reliant' because of cotton-wool parenting. Self-reliance is essential so you can go on to make wise independent choices as an adult. Resilience will allow you to cope with the disappointments and failures that every person must face in life.

Fear of failure can be paralysing. 'A lot of girls I have had contact with are frightened into inaction,' says Lisa Porter. 'They have so many worries about the future that it is as though they are playing a game of chess and rather than risk a pawn, they don't play at all.' A prime example of this is when the time comes for girls to make subject choices. 'They are afraid of making a "wrong" decision, so they take the courses their friends are doing or that their parents recommend, rather than going out on a limb and choosing something they enjoy or would like to try.' Have you ever felt that way?

Drum roll, girls. It's okay to take *informed risks* with your education, just as you need to learn to take informed risks in your lives in general. You need to learn problem-solving and decision-making skills now so that you can be a self-reliant, resilient, well-balanced adult. You will make some mistakes along the way. When you do trip up, you might hear the old 'I told you so'. Those four words are enough to make anyone snap but one way to handle it is to say something like 'Thanks for trying to help but I had to work it out for myself.'

> The worst thing about being a teen girl is people condemning you when you fall when, in fact, you only just tripped and learned something.
>
> Yan, 16

> Don't fear mistakes; they're an investment in learning.
>
> Elizabeth Broderick, Sex Discrimination Commissioner and Commissioner Responsible for Age Discrimination

Take charge of your homework

Girls tell me that many of the arguments they have with their parents are about homework. (That, and the state of their bedrooms!)

You'll probably be thrilled to know I am not a big fan of students having to do lots of homework, particularly in the early high school years. Homework can be highly valuable and stimulating, such as a project where the student is allowed to choose her own topic and explore it in her own way. But I think students are often given homework that is less rewarding than that, because teachers feel pressure to set 'busy work'. This pressure may come from parents who believe that lots of homework means lots of learning.

It concerns me that setting too much homework may create bad work habits by sending you a message that if tasks are not completed during class time they can be completed at home. If we adults managed our time more effectively, perhaps we would not need to take piles of work home to complete, either.

Still, the situation is unlikely to change any time soon. In the first few years of high school, you can expect up to one hour per night of homework, increasing to three and a half hours per night by the end of high school.

There are some parents who think they are helping their daughter cope with her workload by completing her homework or polishing her assignments for her. No good 'collaborate' = to work together

can come from this. The girl may receive good marks for her assignments but will learn nothing – except that she is not smart enough in her parents' eyes and that her best efforts will never be good enough.

If your parents want to give you a hand, tell them there are other ways they can support you. For example, because Teyah and I love reading, we both get excited when she gets a new English novel to study and I read it too, so we can discuss it. You can also ask your parents for any help you need in setting up a good studying environment or developing effective time-management strategies.

Create the right studying environment

The traditional idea of a good studying environment is something akin to a prison: unless a student is in seclusion, in total silence, bent over her books like a slave for hours on end, she isn't really studying. Most girls tell me this approach doesn't work for them. And there are a variety of learning environments, each of which is valid at the right time.

Sometimes, girls (and boys) benefit from learning in a collaborative, interactive way. When a girl is required to sit alone at her desk in her room for hours, she may feel banished and view her isolation as a punishment, which will hardly encourage her to find joy in learning, will it? Many girls I speak to tell me they would prefer to be allowed to be social learners, working with their friends.

When you are in the *understanding* phase of learning about something, it can be a big help to work with other girls outside school. A good example is when girls get together and brainstorm before they commence writing an essay. Another is girls getting together to write summaries of a topic, which they will use later at home on their own when revising.

Nicola Dingle, the director of study skills company Learning Performance, knows more about how to study than anyone else I know. She says that the most effective way to learn *is to teach*. So you might like to get together with other girls and take it in turns to teach topics to the rest of the group. And if you cannot get together with other girls to do this, improvise!

When I was cramming for a test, I would write notes on a blackboard and 'teach' my cuddly toys. (The sad part? I was in high school when I did this *Danni's street cred exits stage left*). But you know what? Not only did Mr Bunny and Scruffy Dog know more about the Ancient Greeks than any other fluffy creatures on the block, I used to nail my tests. Why? Because I had to fully digest the content before I could write up the notes and draw the maps my critters were supposed to be learning.

Another reason why my approach worked? Humour switches on memory. If we are laughing, we are more likely to be able to recall content. That's why even though you may find it hard to remember everything that happened in a lesson, if something amusing happened – like someone told a brilliant joke – you will remember that without any problem! So, by amusing my tragic-little-self while studying and turning it all into a funny game rather than a hard slog, I was really amping up the chances the content would be embedded in my memory.

Studying with a group of friends may also provide an environment that is less threatening than the classroom. This is great if you hesitate to express your opinions in class or aren't receiving much encouragement to. With your study friends, you will have more opportunity to express your views and question others and develop new ways of thinking. Yes, there will be some off-task chit-chat, but that's okay, so long as you are responsible and set clear goals at the outset of your study group meeting. For example, you might all agree that by 4.30 pm you will have identified and discussed the three main themes in the film *Rabbit-Proof Fence*, or whatever it is you are currently studying in class.

Of course, there are times when private work (minus the gags) is essential to completing a task. For example, writing an essay is not a group task.

Importantly, by mixing up your study routine you will also begin recognising which tasks are best done in isolation and which ones are enhanced by discussion with others. The time you do spend studying solo will begin to feel less like a punishment and more like your own smart work choice.

> One time all my friends went to a study group and every time they went they said 'You should have been there, it was awesome. Come with us next time.' This pressured me to go with them and I did and I enjoyed the study group and got a lot out of it.
>
> Frances, 17

> I believe girls work best when they are with other girls they feel comfortable with. It tends to make girls open and imaginative.
>
> Haley, 15

> Girls learn best through discussion. If we aren't participating, we aren't listening!
>
> Anon., 15

> Girls should discuss their ideas and topics for tests together, but study and make notes on their own. I found if I studied with my friends I got nothing done. I had to have peace and quiet for a good two or three days to study at home after school for a test on my own. Then I would share

my understanding by getting together with only one girl, usually a study buddy, and we would go through the syllabus comparing notes.

Frances, 17

You can hold interactive study sessions at home or the local library – or they may be virtual. When you and your friends get home from school, you can call each other and log on together. 'I keep telling Dad I need a bigger monitor, because I end up with so many windows open that I can't always follow what's going on in each one,' says one teenage girl. She and her best friend have about six different things going on at the same time, including multiple instant messaging screens for different friends, a virtual role-playing domain and 'The Palace', an avatar chat room. As well, 'we have our homework open (which I'm pleased to report, we both get done at the end of the night, and it's soooo much more fun doing it this way!),' she says. Not to mention, of course, that they still have phone conversations going on at the same time. Sound familiar?

It might seem alarming to your parents that you and your friends are doing a lot of 'distracting things' while you're meant to be doing you homework. Yet the scene this girl describes also sounds a lot like an average day at the office for most adults. We get our work done despite constant disruptions and the fact that we have to multi-task and keep our co-workers in the loop the whole time.

For example, right now I am writing this chapter, reading my notifications on Facebook, listening to my stepdaughter, Jazmine, tell me she loves me (awww) and texting a friend, who for some bizarre reason has just asked if she can come and eat egg sandwiches with me soon. (When I texted back to say I love a good 'egg sanger', my phone auto-corrected it to read 'egg danger'. Random much? I am now also giggling at the thought of my friend Sassy and I taking on egg dangers . . .)

To a certain extent, then, it's okay for you to grow up learning and working in this way — so long as you know when to shut off distractions and work alone. Later, for example, I will close my office door, let the phone go to voicemail and wait until later to answer emails or check Facebook so I can edit this chapter carefully. Promise!

Reach out for support

'Girls learn best when they have a neat balance of freedom and support,' says Lisa Porter, of Fairfield High School. 'They like to be challenged and have choice in what they do and how they learn, but they also need to feel scaffolded and supported, both in the classroom and at home.'

Girls tend to show greater multi-tasking and organising abilities than boys. They develop time-management skills, such as the ability to do part-time work and still keep up with their study, and have better people skills, particularly an awareness of other people's needs.

There is a risk to being good at these things, though. Being seen as skilled at handling everything, girls are often left to do it all – even though they may end up feeling anxious and overwhelmed. You should never feel that you need to take the whole burden on your shoulders. Don't be left with all the jobs; instead, be assertive, delegate to others and expect other people to do their bit. If you find it difficult to know how to ask other people to share the load, review the Respect Rules in chapter 4, 'Planet Girlfriend'.

❧

Action plan

Pack your own bag of tricks. If you attend lessons, participate in class and complete all your assignments, you are already doing a lot of things right. This will pay off later. Although I mentioned in the introduction that this book was not designed to be a complete guide to being a teen girl and wouldn't cover the practicalities of everything from puberty to passing exams, I do want to sneak in a few of my favourite study tips for you. Because I am cool like that. Thanks to Nicola Dingle for sharing her wisdom:

1 Organise your notes on a regular basis. The best time is when you finish a particular topic or unit of work. Even if the teacher does not ask you to, go through and summarise your notes then. This will save you lots of time closer to exams, when you feel pressured. It also means that if you have missed work or not understood something, you can ask for help while it is still fresh in your (and the teacher's) mind.

2 Spend more time trying to understand the work you find harder or more complicated, rather than only focusing on your favourite subjects or topics. I call this eating your veggies before having your dessert!

3 Use as much variety as possible when studying, for example, make up rhymes or catchy rhythms, use movement, draw pictures and mind maps, and mark your textbooks with coloured pens and highlighters. (Whenever I read a novel for English, I would underline key quotes in different colours, one for each main character. I would also highlight quotes relating to key themes in yellow, and those describing the setting in blue and so on. Later, when it came to writing essays, I could see at a glance where all the good quotes were without having to reread the entire book.) If you engage your five senses, the content will be much easier to remember than if you use words and sentences alone.

4 Because it is difficult to remember something if

you have no interest in it, find something about the information that engages you.

5   Use aided memory techniques. I used to use acronyms to help me recall lists of content. If I had to recall the battles of the Persian War in order, I would use the first letters of the battle names to make up a saying that amused or interested me, so I would find it easier to recall them. For example, Marathon, Thermopylae, Salamis and Plataea became: Marathons Tire Some People (by starting with Marathon, I was off to a head start).

6   Just because you can remember content straight after a study session doesn't mean you will be able to recall it next week when the test is on, or even tomorrow. Much of what you memorise is lost after you finish a memorising session. To help increase your recall, schedule regular revision sessions – at ten minutes, one day and one week after the initial session. If you do this, most of what you are trying to learn will 'stick'.

Learn to manage your workload. If you have trouble getting assignments finished on time, completing homework or revising for exams, sit down and work out ways to get on top of your studies. It can be as simple as making effective use of diaries and calendars, or learning to make lists of your tasks then ticking them off one by one. If you are not sure where to start, ask a parent or favourite teacher to help you.

Develop good study techniques. Most schools provide lessons in study techniques but if you are struggling with how best to do assignments, make summaries or revise for exams, talk to your school to see if they have any extra resources. There are so many books out there on these topics! You may even want to consider using a study skills program outside of the school.

Take informed risks. This is a time when you can explore new fields and see what you are really interested in and good at. You may make a few mistakes along the way or suffer some setbacks, but learning to deal with disappointment is part of growing up.

Learn more about the achievements of learned women. I confess that I once said to my daughter when she was struggling with maths, 'You're just like your mummy. We both love reading and writing but find maths and science tough.' Way to go, Danni. What kind of message was I sending Teyah? The same message Mattel's Barbie gave girls when she spoke her first words in 1994: 'Math is hard!' How limiting.

Throughout history there have been accomplished women across all fields of learning. Seek out textbooks that depict women participating in scientific discoveries, the literary world and political events. What were all those women doing while the men were off exploring, anyway? If you have the option, choose women authors and heroines for your assignments and book projects.

Fifteen years ago, Rachel, who is now a grown woman, was in a class I taught at high school. She says, 'I still remember the first thing I noticed when I walked into your classroom in Year 10: a sticker on the top of the board that said "Girls can be engineers too". Yours was one of the few classrooms where I believed that I could achieve something.' I believe you can *all achieve*.

Get tech savvy. It is essential that all young people have at least basic computing skills. If you are struggling, enrol in a short course privately.

Bring back balance. Some of the learning obstacles girls frequently mention to me are lack of sleep, hunger and stress. To be at your best, you need a good night's sleep, a balanced diet and stress management (for more on that, see the visualisation exercises in the 'Resources' section at the end).

Affirmations
I enjoy learning new things.
I have the potential to achieve and I have faith in my abilities.

8

Career Girl

After appearing on *60 Minutes* one night to talk about the work I do empowering teen girls, I took part in an online chat session with viewers. One concerned person asked me: 'Are you breeding little feminists, though?'

I responded then as I would now: 'I hope so!'

'Feminism' has become the new f-word – an insult word, a word not to be spoken in polite company. All the time, I hear young women say things like 'I'm not a feminist, but ...'

Feminism is the belief that women deserve equality. Is that really so radical a concept that we feel the need to disown it? I asked a group of Year 10 students at a school in Victoria how many of them would describe themselves as feminists. I was truly shocked and saddened when not even one of the hundred or so girls raised her hand!

Perhaps those girls felt that way because women have made such enormous progress towards gaining equality and respect in society. When you enter the workforce, you won't come up against the rigid barriers that existed mere decades ago, when a woman's future was all mapped out for her. School, work for a few years, marriage, babies and housework – for generations of girls that was the plan, whether it was the life they dreamed of or not. You have choices. You have laws against gender discrimination and sexual harassment, and laws protecting a woman's right to keep her job after having a baby.

Believing that the work of feminism is complete in this country, perhaps teen girls feel that the f-word is an embarrassing throwback to the olden days and should be allowed to slip out of our vocabulary.

Not so fast!

You girls *will* still face barriers when you enter the workplace. The same barriers that we have been trying to chip away at, bit by bit, all our adult lives. These are barriers that no government can smash down, no court of law can rule out of existence. They're more shadowy and hard to pin down than that.

The obstacles that you will face exist largely in people's minds. They're the misconceptions that employers have about women and about men. Stereotypes of what is women's work and what is men's. Lack of childcare. Workplaces that don't offer a home/work balance. A deep-seated lack of confidence that holds too many girls and women back from showing their true talents or from negotiating in the workplace as successfully as they could.

These misconceptions and stereotypes are why women's pay still lags behind men's. On average, the weekly pay a woman takes home is 84 per cent of a man's. The imbalance is right there from the beginning: when a young man graduates from a tertiary degree he can expect a median salary of $45,000, while a young woman graduate can expect to start out on $42,000. In senior levels of business, the median wage of a woman chief financial officer is 51 per cent less than a man's. (I had to run my eye back over that figure again, too, certain I'd misread it the first time.)

A clue that may help explain the chasm between men's and women's pay is the fact that women are massively under-represented at the upper levels of the business world. Out of all 200 companies that make up the Australian stock market index known as the ASX 200, there were only six women CEOs in 2006. Finally, and unsurprisingly, women are far more likely than men to be sexually harassed or discriminated against in the workplace.

If wanting to correct these imbalances makes me a feminist, then I am delighted to be called one. My idea of feminism welcomes anyone who supports the idea that women are people with rights and that all people deserve an equal opportunity in life. Guys are definitely invited to join, too.

Finding your own path

You are given a lot of information when considering your options, along with a whole lot of pressure to choose the right subjects at school, the right tertiary course or the right career path. True? Many teenage girls I speak with are overwhelmed about sifting through work and study possibilities, meanwhile weighing up the benefits and pitfalls of taking a part-time job while they are still at school.

This chapter is about what you can do to find your own way through the maze. It looks at what holds some young women back from the career success they deserve and what you can do to find fulfilment in your working life. It celebrates all the amazing talents and qualities this generation of teen girls and women have to offer, and suggests how we can enhance them and share them with the world.

The best part of being a teenage girl is having more responsibilities and finding out about the real outside world.

Jessica, 15

Being a teenage girl gives me the opportunity to begin discovering who I am before I enter the scary, yet hopefully exciting, world of adulthood.

Kirsten, 17

The best part of being a teenage girl is having a whole future and the best part of your life ahead of you.

Amy, 16

Welcome to the boys' club

A high-powered job isn't everyone's cup of tea. Some women choose to devote themselves to parenting full time, which is surely the hardest job on Earth. Others are in the workforce but have no interest in pursuing a senior role. But there are also women who would like to be in the country's boardrooms and in managerial positions but find their careers stalling.

The fact that there are so few women in the upper levels of our workplaces is not simply because they have chosen other roles. In fact, the federal government's Equal Opportunity for Women in the Workplace Agency (EOWA) conducted research among both sexes in the workforce and found that men and women are equally ambitious. Both sexes believe that in their workplaces men progress more quickly than women, that promotions are not always awarded on merit, and that women and men are not treated equally.

In many cases, the Australian workplace is a boys' club. Almost half of all working women think so: 43 per cent. What might surprise you is that the number of men who see their workplace as a boys' club is even greater: 46 per cent.

Women often feel that in order to get recognition they need to work harder than men doing the same job. Excluded from the boys' club, it can be harder for them to progress. One woman surveyed summed up the experience of many women when she said that the men at her work 'stick together to promote each other' while the women were left to 'fight battles on their own'.

The boys' club workplace culture makes it easier for men to get away with discriminating or sexually harassing their female co-workers. We have all heard outrageous stories of harassment and I am betting your mothers have lived through some too: a woman who fails to get a job after an interview and instead scores a come-on from her male interviewer; a woman who gets a promotion only to find it withdrawn when she announces she's pregnant; a woman who is ridiculed when she asks that men take down the porno magazine pictures plastered all over their workspaces.

Bullying and harassment can come at the hands of

women, too. Women's snide comments to other women in the workplace are destructive: 'You must be sleeping with him' or 'It helps that you have great legs,' a woman may say to a female colleague on her promotion. The EOWA survey found that a staggering one in ten women left their last job because they suffered bullying or harassment. Because you don't have as much experience or power in the workplace, teen girls are especially vulnerable.

The need is as great now as it ever was for girls and women to support and stand up for one another in the workplace.

Working mums who never stop working

Almost every adult in the workforce feels they need to spend more time at home with their family than they currently do. They feel burdened by financial responsibilities and demanding workloads that keep them away from the people they love and the non-work activities that keep them sane.

I know this not only from my conversations with other busy working adults, but from research as well. Women are not alone in feeling the ache of wanting to spend more time at home. One survey showed that almost 70 per cent of men feel they don't spend enough time with their children. Another found that 60 per cent feel that they miss out on some of the rewards of being a father because of their jobs.

Despite the fact that both men and women want to spend more time at home with their family, when they are at home, women and men are doing very different things with their time.

Working women are working not only at their job but at home as well. Women continue to do most of the cooking, laundry, nappy-changing, bathing, dressing and grooming of small children, grocery shopping, and the organising of a million and one soccer or netball games, music lessons, birthday parties, school recitals, doctor's appointments and so on in the family. Women with partners spend almost 30 hours each week on household duties.

Their men? They spend around half as much time on housework. Even in couples where both partners work full time, women spend around seven hours more each week on household activities. Emily Maguire writes in her book *Princesses and Pornstars*:

While the professional and legal positions of women have improved enormously in the last half-century, socially and domestically, we've barely progressed at all. We are still judged first on how well we conform to gendered norms that were already looking tattered in 1955. In spite of a need for it, we continually hear that feminism is a thing of the past.

In the social norms she is referring to, women are the homemakers and men are the money makers for the family. Women can get stuck in a self-perpetuating cycle. Carrying a

> 'social norm' = a standard of social behaviour that is expected of the members of a group

greater burden of caring and housework at home, we may have less energy to focus on our careers. Men, expected to take on fewer burdens at home, may have a better chance to take advantage of promotions and new opportunities, possibly leaving their women with even more to do at home.

This has to stop. I get so angry when I am expected to do everything around our house simply because I am the mum. I work (and I am fortunate enough to do work I find very rewarding) yet too many times at home it seems that just because I have a vagina it is assumed I will cook, clean and organise!

I think my children think I am a little crazy when I get so upset about this, but the way I look at it, expecting the woman to do it all – while she works outside the home, too – is not just unfair, it is a political issue. In fact, my teenage girls once went through a very lazy stage and I sent them a three-page letter explaining why I was not going to be the Dobby-style house-elf:

Dear Teyah and Jaz,
Here I am yet again feeling frustrated and angry

about the way in which people are sharing our space.

I'm actually not sure I have fully explained why this is all upsetting me so much so I will do my best to explain. It is not fair to be angry with someone if you haven't given them a full explanation of what you expect first and why it matters to you.

When we are small children it is reasonable to expect our parents will do everything for us, because we can't really safely do all that much for ourselves . . . but as we get older, we learn to contribute and become independent. It's scary but also exciting! . . .

I also think I am teaching you VERY important feminist lessons about how to set limits with people who want to take advantage of you. I am hopefully helping you learn how to set limits with your own families one day so that if they expect to sit around and relax while you run around doing everything, you will be confident enough to tell them that is not fair. I would hate for you to grow up thinking just because you're girls you should be someone's slave . . .

The girls thought I was being a little over-the-top — but really, can you see why this matters?

My point? I think gender equality starts at home. Step up. Be an active member of your household. Trust me, it will not only make you feel independent, it will guarantee you gratitude from your parents.

And don't get caught up in being the 'housewife' when working in groups at school. I have seen many girls offer to tidy up the group's notes for their messier boy partners, or do the majority of the work while their male teammates talk and clown around. Practise setting limits now!

There are pressures on me to balance my very demanding role with parenting. Human rights start at home! I believe doing work I value makes me a better mother and a strong role model for Lucy. I try to make home a guilt-free zone.

Elizabeth Broderick, Sex Discrimination
Commissioner and Commissioner Responsible for
Age Discrimination

Career girl: playground bully, saint or style icon?

I do not buy women's magazines. I gave up that self-destructive little habit some time ago because I got sick of the nasty aftertaste: I really am not coping as well as [insert celebrity mum], am I? Wow, I had no idea I could/

should lose three kilos by next week! Maybe I do need to update my wardrobe . . .

However, on a business trip I decided to dive back into that world and before my flight picked up a copy of *Vive*, a magazine 'for women who mean business'. What sage advice for businesswomen did I find in those 128 pages?

- Fifteen different types of wrinkle cream were advertised or discussed (yes, I counted) including the $930 La Prairie Pure Gold product featuring 'finely ground 24-carat gold'. (Why use gold? Because we can?)

- There was a four-page feature story on Kelly Smythe, a stylist at Channel 7. She sounds like a talented, hard-working woman. My problem with the story was its implication that the main reason Channel 7 was rating well was that the stars now all 'dressed for success' and that Kelly was there to 'keep a check' on how they all looked. Surely there is more to success than just the right pantsuit?

- There was a profile of Carla Bruni. Even though she is an ex-supermodel, France's first lady, a singer-songwriter and an actress, her main claim to fame, according to the magazine, seemed to be that she 'once dated Mick Jagger and Eric Clapton'. *Vive* claimed there was more to Bruni than just her love life – but if so, why did they mention it? Repeatedly.

- The model in the magazine's fashion spread looked no older than 15. She appeared prepubescent and was wearing a seventies-

'tokenism' = a superficial gesture intended to impress and to distract attention from the real issues

inspired playsuit and enormous retro wedges in one shot. Oh, how 'career girl'! By the looks of all that anti-wrinkle-cream advertising, the mag is targeting over-35s — so what was she editor hoping to achieve, other than making her readers feel old and inadequate?

- The recipe section (you know this must be a magazine for *women* who mean business because you won't see a recipe section in the boy's own *Business Review Weekly*) featured silly, fiddly hors d'oeuvres. What working woman has time to whip up 'Iberico ham and quail-egg tarts'? I particularly resented the magazine's guilt-loaded message that crackers and cheese were now a definite no-no and that even 'risotto balls are considered passé.' Blimey, don't come here for nibbles, then.

I could go on and on. Don't even get me started on the tokenistic story on what feminism means today, buried up on page 114 and entitled 'The F-word'.

The f-word that came to mind for me when reading this magazine was . . . frivolous.

Success in the business world is not about having youthful skin, a stick-thin figure, name-droppable boyfriends, stylish clothes and the ability to whip up a marvellous quail-egg tart. So where are the images in popular culture of *real* successful business and career women?

Boys are saturated with images of working men to model themselves on, in movies, children's stories, novels, TV shows, news coverage, ads. They have had fathers from generation to generation passing down their expectations of the kind of working man they are to be.

But women are, to a large extent, still making up the working-woman identity as we go along. This can lead us to inadvertently set up our own traps to be snared in at work. With few role models and little advice, women may one minute try to live up to their imaginary idea of a hard-nosed businesswoman, then revert to playground cattiness.

We may fall back on the old lessons we were taught as girls, when we got rewarded for being sugar and spice and all things nice. Women are often expected to be humble, selfless and passive – and that can put us at a disadvantage in the workplace. So I don't fall into that trap, above my desk I display a quote from Marianne Williamson's classic book *A Return to Love*:

> There is nothing enlightening about shrinking so that other people will not feel insecure around you . . . and

as we let our light shine, we unconsciously give other people permission to do the same. As we are liberated from our own fear, our presence liberates others.

It is important for all of us – women and girls – to be proud of our talents and abilities, and become more comfortable discussing our achievements. This will help you in your career and life. It will also encourage other girls to be upfront about their skills, which will assist them in being more assertive, too. It is okay to actively promote yourself – in fact, it is essential if you are to reach your full potential.

Women in the workplace tend to find it difficult to assert their worth to others. We find it tough to tell our employers and other workplace power players that we deserve recognition, respect, a raise or a promotion. We fear looking vain or like a diva, and worry that we'll be perceived as a bitch or full of ourselves. We hate to risk being disliked. Advertisers know women tend to like wearing good clothes and bling because they signal to the world 'Hey, I'm worth it!' Yet at work, we have trouble telling employers and colleagues exactly that: I am skilled and experienced and deserve your respect.

We are living in a highly competitive business era in which there is intense competition for jobs. It will only become more important that you feel comfortable about promoting your skills and negotiating with others. You don't know your market value until you ask, and expect, to be paid well for good work.

∽

The entitled generation

If only finding the right career was a matter of decid-ing what we want to be then clicking our ruby-red heels together Dorothy style. Finding a job that suits us and gives us a sense of fulfilment and satisfaction can be a long journey. There may be twists and turns, long, flat boring plains, splendid, scenic peaks and dismal chasms.

Along the way, we inevitably have to do our share of dull tasks and learn many lessons. Then maybe forget them and learn them all over again. Even if we get our dream job, we may find that it wasn't really our destina-tion at all but only a detour. Suddenly we may have a different goal and completely different things to learn.

Most women my age learnt these truths early on, way back when we got a part-time job during high school. I find the expectations of some of you are quite different, though. Some girls I meet now have a sense of entitlement more suited to a 30-something executive. I meet girls who can't see why they should have to start out at the bottom and work their way up. Not all girls – but enough to get my antennae twitching.

I can honestly say that I have loved every job I ever had,

including working as a babysitter, restaurant waitress and at McDonald's. Each job has taught me something valuable. At McDonald's, for instance, I learnt how to work in a team, motivate and train colleagues, and look after customers. I also developed a strong work ethic there, because the job demanded that I work hard.

Girls with a feeling of entitlement believe they shouldn't need to do such gritty starter jobs because it's beneath them. What they don't realise is how much they are missing out on. They will lag behind other girls in learning skills crucial to success in the workplace later on. And their attitude may be a big turn-off to potential employers.

Mia Freedman, who became editor of *Cosmopolitan* at 24, didn't just roll out of bed into a great outfit and killer heels then step into that position, as too many girls feel they should be able to. She started her career doing work experience as an ambitious 19-year-old, and was happy to fetch the mail and get coffee at first. If she had the chance to fill in for the receptionist at lunch, she was rapt, happy simply to be there 'breathing the air'. When she did become an editor, she made a special effort with other young people who came in for work experience looking for a way into the competitive world of magazine publishing. 'I insisted we have a structured program to give them a well-rounded understanding of how a magazine worked,' she writes.

Inevitably, this included some boring tasks because – *guess what, kids* – there are many, many boring tasks to be done in every workplace. At every level.

Over the years, I began to notice a change in attitude from some (not all) of the work experience students. Gratitude was being replaced with a sense of entitlement and absurd expectations.

Years later, after leaving the magazine game, she was flicking through the newspaper one morning and was shocked to see she'd been mentioned in an article featuring other magazine editors:

The gist of the story was that the magazine industry was apparently in a 'tizz' about some anonymous rumours on a website.

One of these rumours – are you sitting down? – was that *'Mia Freedman once sent a work experience person out to buy her son a banana.'*

This is but one of many examples of work experience students and junior staff getting annoyed when asked to do tasks they feel are beneath them. One of Mia's friends asked a young person to help a fashion assistant carry some clothes. They refused, delivering the immortal line 'I have a degree, I'm not a Sherpa.'

There is good self-esteem – and then there is

preciousness that seems more like narcissism. You need to have a strong sense of self-worth, but not at the expense of a ground-

'narcissism' = extreme admiration for oneself; an exaggerated feeling of self-importance

ing in reality. Most career women at the top of their game have years of hard slogging, networking and persistence behind them. Fact.

Even women in industries considered glamorous have had to put in their time doing work that is anything but glamorous. Melinda Nielsen is one of Australia's premier make-up artists and styles major celebrities. 'Long before I even studied make-up you could find me working on the make-up counters,' she says. 'Those years were truly my foundation for what I am doing now. It's where I really learnt my craft because . . . it gave me a vast array of experience not only with applying make-up but also in building relationships with people.' After gaining qualifications, many of her fellow students didn't know where to go from there and floundered, struggling to find a foothold in the highly competitive industry.

'I hold a personal belief that you become like the people you hang around,' says Melinda, 'so I found people who were successful . . . I began to assist with some of the top make-up artists in Australia. I did whatever it took to be in their world – I cleaned brushes, carried bags and got some fantastic opportunities. I started making my own contacts and building relationships, and that launched me into my career.'

Sophie York, barrister, lecturer, author and mother of four, says, 'One of my first jobs was as a shopkeeper . . . I was pressured initially to do work as a paralegal yet I have no regrets over my choice, as through this starter role I learnt so much about human nature and people. Working where I did, I was exposed to a side of life I had had limited contact with previously – homeless people, drug addicts – and it helped me develop a stronger sense of compassion and empathy, which I brought to my later work in the legal profession.'

Hard junior-level work is not necessarily a bad thing. Even tasks that seem 'beneath' you can teach you valuable skills, let alone impress employers who are looking for staff with a good attitude. However, do not allow yourself to be exploited. If you are asked to do things that make you feel uncomfortable or that are dangerous or simply inappropriate, you should question such requests and set boundaries.

❧

Which career?

Only you can make the tough decisions about what you want to do when you leave school, but adults can be a helpful resource. Ask your parents to offer up their experiences at work – good and bad.

If you know someone who has a job you're interested in, see if you can set up a time to meet with them. Ask them how they got into the field and what the pros and cons are. Hands-on experience is the best way to learn about a job – and it looks good on a CV – so if there is a chance for you to do some work at their workplace, whether paid or unpaid, try it.

The activities you enjoy outside of school, such as sports and hobbies, can be a useful clue for the kind of work you will be suited to.

Getting to know what you aren't interested in is just as valuable. One of the key lessons I have learnt is that just because you *can* do something, it doesn't mean you *should*. This is a trap that young women fresh out of school can be easily led into: flattered to be offered a great job, they do it even though their heart and soul are somewhere else. Other girls take a place in a highly sought-after course at university, such as medicine, simply because they got the marks and are excited that they won that race.

Melinda Nielsen notes that 'it is very important to be talented at what you do, but it will never be enough to succeed in a competitive field. Firstly, I think you need to have a passion for what you are doing, otherwise you will lose hope when the setbacks start to come. If you are passionate about something, you will want to persevere with it and won't give up when it gets tough'.

So don't neglect the signs of what jobs are uninspiring

for you, too. If you try your hand at a part-time job or a work-experience placement and really don't like or do well at it, ask yourself what it was about the work that was a turn-off. This can help you pinpoint the right career.

Don't overlook the resources available at school and in the community, too. Making a time to speak to your school career adviser can be a great place to start, as can attending career expos.

⁂

What if you want to leave school early?

When I was in high school, about a third of the students left at the end of Year 10 to work full-time. The majority of my friends left at this point and went on to have fabulous careers. However, the world has definitely changed since then and satisfying full-time job opportunities for early school leavers just don't exist any more. Most teenagers can find only part-time work and people aged 15 to 24 have almost three times the level of unemployment of those aged 24 to 54. Today, young people should aim to complete their first year of senior schooling or an equivalent vocational qualification, as an absolute minimum.

You may complain that the learning you do at school is not relevant and think that you will be happier in the 'real world'. There *are* many 'unreal' elements to schooling – but it is those very elements that can be of enormous benefit. School is a generally nurturing environment that allows you to make mistakes; the real world is not always so kind.

Students who were desperate to leave school often come back to visit a few months later and say they are filled with regret about their decision as they feel lost and lonely in their new workplace. They miss their friends and being able to interact with other young people all day.

'I think for girls who leave school early it is challenging, as they don't really fit in anywhere,' says Leigh, whose daughter left early to go to business college. 'Her school friends all bonded over exams and playground gossip, which of course she was no longer a part of, whilst the other girls she worked with in the office [were] much older ... For a while there, she didn't seem to fit socially anywhere.'

In the end, the choice is in your hands. If you are adamant about leaving school early, consider combining school studies with some practical, paid training. There are a number of Vocational Education and Training (VET) programs that can be studied at school or by correspondence.

❦

What skills are important in the workplace?

You are likely to move through several different careers in your working life. This means that to succeed in the workplace, you need to make sure you develop the basic skills and qualities that employers across a broad spectrum of jobs will always look for.

The 8 Employability Skills

- **Communication** – listening and understanding other staff and customers; speaking and writing clearly; being assertive
- **Learning** – applying learning to practical situations; being willing to learn in any setting; managing your own learning
- **Technology** – having basic technology skills; being willing to learn about new technology
- **Teamwork** – working well with people of different ages, gender, race and religion; working well as an individual and as a team member
- **Planning and organising** – managing time and priorities; coordinating with others; planning; collecting and organising information
- **Problem solving** – developing creative, innovative solutions to problems; using mathematics to solve problems
- **Self-management** – managing your own time and priorities; taking initiative; making decisions
- **Enterprise** – adapting to new situations; being resourceful and creative; identifying new opportunities

The personal qualities employers prize the most are loyalty, reliability, commitment, honesty, integrity, enthusiasm, a sense of justice and care for others, the ability to deal with pressure, motivation, adaptability, good personal presentation, common sense, positive self-esteem and a sense of humour.

Young people wanting to start their own businesses need to understand more than just the mechanics of the corporate world; they need confidence to use their whole, creative selves in their working lives, to employ their hopes and aspirations, to pursue their passions. Creativity is the central, challenging part of business . . .

I'd also like to see entrepreneurial — as distinct from managerial — skills taught to young people. But above all we have a responsibility to teach children to think critically, to distinguish information from entertainment, advertisement and political propaganda, and to trust and develop their intuitive selves.

Leanne Preston, founder of the company
Wild Child, and 2007 Telstra Australian
Business Woman of the Year

It is because of the relationships that I've built that I've had most of the opportunities and open

*doors throughout my career. Be genuine in your
dealings with people. Most people have a pretty
good radar for detecting a fake. So be real. Treat
people the way you would like to be treated, even
if it's difficult to do so. This will build in you
resilience and strength of character, which are
always great qualities to have.*

Melinda Nielsen, make-up artist

❧

Action plan

Start an Employability Skills Portfolio. This is a
record of the ways in which you have demonstrated the 8
Employability Skills listed above at school, at home or in
part-time work, both paid and unpaid. I suggest you start
thinking about this as early as possible and set it up as a
document you can update regularly.

For example, under 'Planning and organising', you
could note:

+ a school group assignment in which you had to
  allocate tasks to the other group members;
+ forming a band outside of school, for which you
  recruited new members; and
+ organising a children's birthday party at your part-
  time job at a fast-food chain.

Regularly updating a skills portfolio will increase your confidence. And when the time comes for you to apply for work, you will have evidence of your achievements and skills

'emotional intelligence' = a measure of a person's self-awareness, generosity, personal motivation, empathy and ability to love and be loved by friends and family

at your fingertips. If you know the skills employers are looking for, and have evidence that you have developed those skills, you are able to speak the same language when you go to a job interview.

Oh, and guess what? Doing your share of family chores is not only a decent thing to do but also a great way to develop your teamwork, planning and organising skills. (Yep, I am obsessed with getting young people to help out at home aren't I? Such. A. Mum.)

When I look at the skills portfolios of the girls I work with, I feel optimistic about their opportunities. Many of the skills and personal attributes employers look for relate to emotional intelligence, which research has shown females tend to be high in. We are naturally inclined to have strong relationship skills and to be good at managing our emotions and those of others. So developing better self-esteem and assertiveness not only helps us feel better about ourselves, it helps make us more employable!

Nurture your growing independence. An alarming number of parents look for jobs for their teenage children, scouring job boards and making calls on their children's behalf. Please don't be tempted to let your parents do this for you. You need to learn to become independent and manage your career yourself. If you are going to fumble or stumble, it is better that you do so now, not in your twenties, when the stakes are higher. And imagine if you were an employer and received a call from a candidate's mum. It's unlikely you would think of that teen as mature or high in initiative.

Put together a great CV. Employers may get hundreds of applications when they advertise a position. They do not want to wade through too much information and they don't want a CV that's difficult to read. A CV should be no longer than two pages and typed in a simple 12-point font, in black and white. You should include the following points on your CV.

Key CV points

+ **Contact details** – If you have a fun-sounding email address such as partyprincess@hotmail.com.au, set up a second, more professional one you can use for job applications.
+ **Career objective** – This should be a few simple

words, such as 'To be employed in a stimulating environment where I can make a positive contribution and share my enthusiasm for learning and working with others'.

+ **Education** – First should come your current year of schooling and the subjects you are studying. Then you should list any training courses you have completed, e.g. first aid, word processing.

+ **Awards** – These should include not only academic achievements but any significant awards for extracurricular activities, such as sport or dance.

+ **Employment** – All paid and unpaid jobs or work experience should be listed.

+ **Interests** – Think carefully about how you describe your interests, e.g. 'live music and dancing' sounds much better than 'going to parties'.

+ **Key skills** – The key skills mentioned in the job advertisement should be addressed here. This is where the Employability Skills Portfolio proves invaluable, as you can refer back to it. For example, if the ad mentions that applicants need strong communication skills, one of the points in the 'Key skills' section of the CV might read:

Communication
At school I have participated in a wide variety of activities that have helped me develop both my

written and my verbal communication skills, including debating, public speaking, letter writing and producing essays. While working as a volunteer for the RSPCA, I assisted in handing out pamphlets to members of the public and advised them on how to best care for their pets. The staff at the RSPCA always enjoyed talking to me and I liked explaining information to pet owners of various ages and backgrounds.

• **Referees** – Supply contact details of two or three responsible adults who can vouch for you in a workplace (in a paid or unpaid position), at school or in a group you belong to such as a sporting or debating team.

Don't neglect the cover letter. The cover letter is the first impression an employer has of you. Like your CV, it needs to be clear and simple, not busy or decorated. It should be concise and to the point – definitely no longer than a page – and should briefly illustrate how you fulfil the requirements listed in the job ad.

If the job ad doesn't include the name of a contact person, call the organisation and find the name of the person who will be making the hiring decision, then address the cover letter to that person. When that is not possible, avoid the informal 'Hi' and use instead 'Dear Human Resources' or 'Dear Hiring Manager'.

Prepare for the job interview. The key is preparation. A checklist may help you feel more organised and on top of everything when you go to the interview.

Pre-interview checklist

* **Learn about the company** – What does the organisation make or sell, or what service does it provide?
* **Learn about the job** – What will you be required to do in the job and where does the role fit into the organisation?
* **Get your employment file ready** – Make sure you have a presentation folder to take with you to the interview, containing:
  o CV
  o Cover letter you sent to apply for this job
  o Qualifications and school records
  o Certificates or special awards relevant to the job
  o Written references, if you have them
  o Samples of your work or hobbies that may be related to the job
* **Know how to get there**
  o Double-check the address of the organisation
  o Look up how to get there
  o Check public transport timetables or parking options, aiming to arrive at least ten minutes early

- ○ If in doubt, do a trial run and time how long it takes
- **Plan how you'll present yourself**
  - ○ Decide what you are going to wear and have it ready the night before. Dress to suit the occasion. Avoid wearing 'way out' clothes, scruffy jeans or thongs
  - ○ Be clean, neat and tidy. Brush your hair, have clean fingernails (no chipped nail polish) and clean shoes
- **Practise your answers** – Be prepared to give brief, clear answers to questions that employers commonly ask in interviews:
  - ○ What aspects of the job interest you most?
  - ○ What do you consider your special skills and abilities are?
  - ○ Have you had any work experience in this type of work?
  - ○ What do you know about our company?
  - ○ Are you active in any clubs or community organisations?
  - ○ What are your leisure activities, hobbies or interests?
  - ○ Which of your school subjects interested you the most?
  - ○ What are your long-term career plans?
  - ○ Would you undertake further training if it was required for this position?
  - ○ How do you cope with new situations and procedures?

- How do you feel about working as part of a team?
- Would you be prepared to work overtime or on weekends if required?
- When could you start?

♦ **Practise your questions** – If invited by the employer to ask questions, ask job-related questions rather than, say, questions about holidays or pay. This creates a good impression and lets the employer know you are eager to work for the company. Examples include:

- What would my career prospects be?
- What further study could I do?
- Where and whom would I be working with?
- Is any training given with the position?

Ace the job interview. Unless you have nerves of steel, there is a good chance you will feel nervous and a little uncertain. Even adults feel nervous during a job interview, you know! I interviewed a woman for a role once and she actually started crying she was so scared. (I had to get her some water, a tissue and make extra-special smiley faces at her to calm her down.) These tips may help.

Job interview tips

♦ Arrive ten minutes early, to give yourself time to gather your thoughts and check your appearance.
♦ Switch off your mobile phone.

- Introduce yourself to the receptionist. Give your name, time of the appointment and the name of the person who is interviewing you. Speak clearly and politely. When the receptionist tells you where to wait, thank them and wait quietly.
- Greet the interviewer(s) and introduce yourself.
- Smile and be ready to shake hands.
- Enter the interviewer's office and wait to take the seat that is offered to you
- Maintain eye contact, as this shows you are listening and that you are confident and trustworthy.
- Though you may be nervous, make sure you keep your hands and legs still. Don't fidget or fiddle. Don't even think about smoking or chewing gum!
- Answer questions honestly, politely and clearly, and in sufficient detail.
- Always try to turn the question to your advantage. This is your opportunity to show you have the skills, interests and experience to do the job.
- Don't be shy about your achievements. No achievement is too small to mention, if it is relevant to a question that the interviewer has asked.
- If you don't understand a question, ask for clarification. That is better than giving an irrelevant answer.
- Try not to punctuate your sentences with 'umm' or 'err' or 'like'. Taking a short pause to think about the

question is perfectly acceptable and makes a much better impression.

+ At the end of the interview, politely thank the interviewer(s).

Review progress after every interview. It may seem that a job interview is a win–lose proposition. Get the job = win. Get knocked back = lose. A more helpful way to look at an unsuccessful job interview is as a learning opportunity. After each interview, evaluate your performance. What did you do well? What could you improve on next time? An unsuccessful interview is not a waste of time but an experience you can reflect on to help in future interviews.

Make the most of work experience. You won't be given the most challenging or glamorous tasks during work experience. If you're at a law firm, you won't be standing up in court saying 'I object!' but you may well be fetching the mail or tidying up the boardroom.

Nevertheless, by being proactive you can get the maximum value out of your work experience. If you find yourself shunted to the Siberian outer reaches of the office, given nothing constructive to do, you can approach the person who is supervising your work experience and politely say something such as 'I would really like to build on my employment skills this week. Is there anything you would like me to do that could help me develop them?' If you take a copy of the 8 Employability Skills, it will give the work experience supervisor something concrete to go on.

Don't reject volunteer work as a valuable means of gaining experience and making connections. Sophie York firmly believes some of the early unpaid opportunities she embraced not only allowed her to network with mentors but also eventually led her to interesting, well-paid positions.

'One of the things I think is really invaluable in the early days is to seek out other people who have gone before you,' says Sophie. 'In the workplace it can be hard to find people who have the time to be nurturing, so I sought mentors through volunteer positions that connected me with retired professionals who had been there, done that.

'The key, too, is to think: What can I offer? What can I contribute? Don't make money the priority – make learning and service the priority. If you do this, the money will come. For example, early on in my career I volunteered as a magistrate at a university for their students' mock trial exercises. This later led to the offer of paid lecturing work at that university, which in turn led to other wonderful things, too.'

Sit at the table. Facebook's chief operating officer Sheryl Sandberg thinks more women will succeed in the workplace if they (a) get more help at home with the chores so they have more time and energy to devote to their careers (Amen, sista!) and (b) sit at the table. What she means is that women need to put themselves forward for leadership opportunities so they can practise being in charge *and let others see* they want responsibilities. They need to put their hands up more in class. They need to volunteer for tasks. They need to actively seek ways of letting others know they have valuable contributions to make.

Get amongst it, girls!

Affirmations

I have many skills and talents to offer the world. Whatever work I choose to do, I do it well and learn from it.

Resources

Visualisation exercises

During a visualisation exercise, you relax and go on a guided imaginative journey. The aim is to put your body and mind in a state of calm and control. It is a way of developing controlled breathing and imagination, and of promoting a positive outlook. When you take the time out to be calm and focus on your inner thoughts and your breath, you reinforce the connection between your mind and your body.

Visualisation exercises are not just mystical. The effectiveness of visualisation has been well documented. Professional athletes mentally rehearse peak performances and cancer patients use visualisation techniques to help regain their health.

I have spoken to many teen girls who have had great success using visualisation activities before bedtime, as part of a ritual to help them unwind and settle for sleep. Often teenagers do not sleep well. In fact, many of you are considered to be sleep deprived. Developing soothing, positive routines before bed helps you form new sleep patterns.

There are many types of visualisation activities. Here I offer two basic guided visualisations for you to try. The first is designed to help you face the daily stresses in your life, such as at school. The second focuses on helping you deal with bullying and intimidation.

I recommend that you or someone else read the visualisation instructions out aloud and make a recording that you can play back regularly to guide you through the exercise. Alternatively, you can have someone read the instructions to you as you do the exercise.

The instructions should be read in a slow, soothing voice. The reader should pause regularly, allowing you to focus on what you can see, hear and feel. Calming music or sounds – such as gentle rain or the ocean – may be played in the background. A candle may be lit or essential oils burnt, to create a full sensory experience. Bliss!

Visualisation exercises are best done in a quiet place where you can completely relax, lying flat on your back with your arms by your side, or sitting comfortably with your shoulders back – not hunched – to allow for deep breathing. Wear loose clothing and make sure that you are comfortable, neither too cold nor too warm.

You may wish to use some of the affirmations spread throughout the previous chapters to create your own visualisation exercises. There are many excellent visualisation and meditation CDs that you may wish to try, too. For younger girls, I like *Indigo Dreaming* by Indigo Kidz, *Butterfly Dreaming* by Denise Allen and *The Rainbow Collection* by Petrea King. For older teens, Denise Allen's *Cool Karma* is excellent and Petrea King has a very good series of CDs suitable for both adults and older girls, which focus on relaxation, self-esteem, forgiveness, improving sleep and more.

About stress

When you dwell on your fears and anxieties, your thoughts have a physical impact on your body. The human nervous system has difficulty distinguishing between a real danger, such as a dog coming to attack you, and an imagined danger, such as a school assignment that is nearly due. If we mentally react to the assignment deadline as though it were a dangerous crisis, our body responds as if it were, by preparing to either fight off the perceived danger or flee from it. This is known as the 'fight or flight' response. There is also actually a third stress response: freezing. We can be quite literally immobilised by our fears and anxieties.

The immediate physical effects of stress include increased heart rate, rapid and shallow breathing, a dry mouth and dilated pupils. Temporary stress can be helpful. It can motivate us to overcome challenges, such as getting that assignment in on time. And if we are in fact in physical danger, stress ensures our body responds by virtually shutting down non-essential functions, such as digestion, and becoming tense and ready for action.

However, ongoing stress has serious health implications, including headaches, disrupted sleep, nightmares, increased or decreased appetite, fatigue and nervous indigestion. One of the most noticeable physical symptoms of stress is tension in your muscles.

Because your mind is not separate from your body, ongoing stress changes the way you feel and act, too. It causes inability to concentrate, boredom, loss of willpower, poor time management, overreaction to mistakes, uncontrollable emotional outbursts and the increased consumption of alcohol, tobacco or other drugs.

The following visualisation exercise allows you to rehearse what it feels like to have the ability and desire to handle potentially stressful situations with calmness and a positive attitude. Regularly practising this exercise will help you develop new, more positive self-talk so you can respond calmly and optimistically to life's inevitable challenges and setbacks. You cannot always control the events that you experience, but you can control how you respond.

In the first part of the exercise, you will relax your muscles and slow down your breathing, easing the physical symptoms of stress and putting you in a calm frame of mind to begin your visualisation.

Stress visualisation

Gently shut your eyes. Focus only on your breathing. You do not need to change your breathing, just become aware of your breath: in through your nose, and out through your mouth. Long, slow, steady, deep breaths. Feel your chest rise and fall. Listen to the sound of your breath.

Although you will hear other sounds, simply notice them and let them fade from your attention. Focus on the sound of your own breathing. This is your time to relax, to feel good, to be still.

As other thoughts enter your mind, let them pass. Focus only on the present and on your senses.

Visualise the toes on your left foot and imagine each one uncurling. Let go of all tension and feel each toe become soft and relaxed. Allow this feeling to travel along the sole of your foot, to the heel. Now your entire left foot feels relaxed. Every joint is loose. And your breath is slow, long and deep. With each breath you feel more and more relaxed. Calmer.

Focus now on the lower half of your left leg. Feel it sink into the floor, relaxed. Feel this sensation spread up into your knee, which now loosens, and into your thigh. Your whole left leg is warm and relaxed. All you are focused on is your own body and the sound of your breath. You do not allow any other thoughts to disturb your calm. You merely notice them and then let them go.

Bring your awareness to your right foot. Imagine each toe slowly uncurling. Focus on the muscles in your right foot, your lower leg and up into your thigh, until both legs are deeply relaxed.

There is absolutely no tension in your lower body. You feel good. You feel safe.

Soften and release the muscles in your buttocks, too. You feel relaxed and warm.

Now visualise the fingers on your left hand opening. Feel each finger unclench and relax. Imagine each part of your hand softening. Allow this feeling to spread up into your wrist. Feel your hand and wrist loosen. Feel the sensation spread into your elbow. Into your shoulder. Feel your shoulder roll back and drop as you release any tension.

And now visualise this deep relaxation in the fingers of the right hand, the right wrist, the right elbow, the right shoulder.

Both left and right hands and arms are relaxed.

Focus now on your stomach. Feel the muscles in your abdomen soften.

Feel this wave of relaxation spread through your body, into your spine. Allow each vertebra in your spine to loosen. With each breath your body feels more, and still more, relaxed.

Focus now on your neck. Release any tension. Now your face. Feel each line in your brow smoothen. Your lips and teeth gently part as the mouth softens, too. No tightness.

Your whole body is now completely relaxed. And you feel good. And you feel safe and warm.

Breathe.

Now, imagine you have just woken in the morning. The sunlight falls from your window onto your face and fills you with a sense of calm. You feel protected.

The light spreads this warmth from your face right through your entire body. Become aware of being filled with a sense of joy. Bask in this golden, healing light.

Picture yourself getting out of bed and getting ready to go to school. You do not rush. You are organised. You are on time. You feel calm and in control.

You feel positive about the day ahead. You know you have all the skills you will need to complete your tasks for the day. You have faith in your abilities.

Take a moment to think about the skills and attributes you have that will ensure you have a successful day. What are you good at? What do you enjoy doing?

Picture yourself leaving for school.

Imagine now that you are about to begin a task you usually find difficult and stressful.

You may still feel some stress, but you know these feelings are not necessarily negative. Stress can also be motivating and can encourage you to extend yourself. You have no reason to fear the task before you, because you are prepared. You have set yourself up for success. What preparation did you do so that you can respond differently this time?

Visualise yourself engaged in the task, succeeding at it.

How does it feel to respond calmly and optimistically in this situation?

And as you leave the experience and become focused again on your body in the here and now, take a moment to think about what you have learnt from this exercise. Take a deep breath, open your eyes and come back to the present.

You may now wish to write about your observations. How might your life change if you face difficult situations more calmly and optimistically?

About bullying and intimidation

As little girls, many of us were taught to be quiet and compliant, to be 'seen and not heard', to play 'nice'. But passivity can make us vulnerable to being bullied.

Research tells us that most bullies are, despite their intimidating front, often actually weak and insecure and have low self-confidence. That is why they resort to intimidation and violence to get what they want. That is why they pick targets they think are weaker than they are.

I encourage you to practise standing up for yourself and letting the world know when you are not comfortable and your boundaries are being crossed. This is not about being aggressive, but assertive. You need to show – through the words you choose, your tone of voice and your body language – that you expect to be listened to, and to have your opinions heard and respected. When you communicate assertively, you show that you have confidence and inner strength.

It can take years to gain true self-confidence and inner strength, but there is solid evidence that we can speed the process up by practising assertive behaviours – that is, by following the 'fake it till you make it' principle.

When I first started teaching, I worked in a very challenging school. I quickly saw that students completely ignored or taunted the teachers who showed weakness. Teachers who were aggressive were hated and would often provoke emotional and sometimes physical outbursts from their students, many of whom came from homes where there was violence. These students had been brought up to attack before being attacked.

Although I was at times fearful and worried, I knew I had to look as if I was in control and speak with authority. Faking it worked for me in those early days. Before I knew it, I was no longer merely pretending that I knew how to manage the class. I was managing my class.

The next visualisation activity explores the idea that you can bolster your inner strength by getting in touch with your inner assertive Amazon. Early Greek literature contains many references to strong women, including the Amazons, a race of revered warrior women. In this visualisation you will first imagine your inner Amazon and then picture yourself dealing assertively with a bullying or intimidating person. The aim is to help you develop the strength to be assertive when you face such a situation in real life.

Bullying and intimidation visualisation

Gently shut your eyes. Focus only on your breathing. You do not need to change your breathing, just become aware of your breath: in through your nose, and out through your mouth. Long, slow, steady, deep breaths. Feel your chest rise and fall. Listen to the sound of your breath.

Although you will hear other sounds, simply notice them and let them fade from your attention. Focus on the sound of your own breathing. This is your time to relax, to feel good, to be still.

As other thoughts enter your mind, let them pass. Focus only on the present and on your senses.

Visualise the toes on your left foot and imagine each one uncurling. Let go of all tension and feel each toe become soft and relaxed. Allow this feeling to travel along the sole of your foot, to the heel. Now your entire left foot feels relaxed. Every joint is loose. And your breath is slow, long and deep. With each breath you feel more and more relaxed. Calmer.

Focus now on the lower half of your left leg. Feel it sink into the floor, relaxed. Feel this sensation spread up into your knee, which now loosens, and into your thigh. Your whole left leg is warm and relaxed. All you are focused on is your own body and the sound of your breath. You do not allow any other thoughts to disturb your calm. You merely notice them and then let them go.

Bring your awareness to your right foot. Imagine each

toe slowly uncurling. Focus on the muscles in your right foot, your lower leg and up into your thigh, until both legs are deeply relaxed.

There is absolutely no tension in your lower body. You feel good. You feel safe.

Soften and release the muscles in your buttocks, too. You feel relaxed and warm.

Now visualise the fingers on your left hand opening. Feel each finger unclench and relax. Imagine each part of your hand softening. Allow this feeling to spread up into your wrist. Feel your hand and wrist loosen. Feel the sensation spread into your elbow. Into your shoulder. Feel your shoulder roll back and drop as you release any tension.

And now visualise this deep relaxation in the fingers of the right hand, the right wrist, the right elbow, the right shoulder.

Both left and right hands and arms are relaxed.

Focus now on your stomach. Feel the muscles in your abdomen soften.

Feel this wave of relaxation spread through your body, into your spine. Allow each vertebra in your spine to loosen. With each breath your body feels more, and still more, relaxed.

Focus now on your neck. Release any tension. Now your face. Feel each line in your brow smoothen. Your lips and teeth gently part as the mouth softens, too. No tightness.

Your whole body is now completely relaxed. And you feel good. And you feel safe and warm.

Breathe.

Imagine you are strolling along a beach. The sand is golden. Gentle waves are splashing at the shoreline. The sun is warm on your shoulders. The sky is blue and there are white fluffy clouds floating past. You feel safe, warm, happy. Listen to the sound of the waves as they lap against the shore.

You see a woman walking towards you. You know this is your inner Amazon, coming to meet you. You smile as you recognise her. You trust her and feel safe with her.

Your inner Amazon is strong. She can fight to protect you. Yet she is so sure of her own power that she does not even need to exert it. Her mere presence sends a signal that she is a woman to revere.

Your inner Amazon walks tall. Her shoulders are back. She is confident, powerful looking. Look at her closely. What does she look like? What is she wearing? Look into her eyes and see that there is no fear in them.

When she approaches you, she is happy to see you. Imagine how she greets you.

She promises that she will always be with you, that she will defend you and remind you of your own power. For she is you, a special part of you. She will always keep you safe.

Listen to her tone when she speaks. Notice the words she chooses to use.

She reminds you again of your own power and the power of all girls. What does she tell you about your own power?

She leads you by the hand to a pool of water. She asks you to look at your reflection. You see that she and you have now merged. You are now the Amazon.

How do you now stand? How do you sound? How do you feel?

You know that you will take care of yourself and keep yourself safe. You know that you have the courage to set boundaries.

Imagine that you now see a person who used to intimidate you coming towards you. Observe their behaviour but choose not to let it upset you. You respond to them calmly and assertively. They are surprised by your new approach and change the way they respond to you.

Listen to how you sound when you talk to them. What words do you use? Observe how you stand.

How does it feel to respond calmly and assertively in this situation?

When I count slowly to three, you will leave the scene, taking with you the feeling of safety, confidence and inner strength.

One . . . two . . . three.

And as you leave the experience and become focused again on your body in the here and now, take a moment to think about what you have learnt from this exercise. Take a deep breath, open your eyes and come back to the present.

You may now wish to write about your observations. What might change in your life if you become more assertive?

I adapted the idea of an inner Amazon from the work of Anita Roberts, whose Safeteen program is aimed at eliminating violence in the lives of young people across North America.

Useful websites, organisations, books and magazines

Enlighten Education

My gifts to you:
FREE iPhone app, The Butterfly Effect: Get your daily dose of awesome, delivered straight to your iPhone.

+ Affirmation – messages to boost self-esteem and body image
+ Inspiration – wise words from amazing women
+ Information – web links to info every girl needs to know

FREE wallpapers for your phone: Make your phone not just pretty but also positive, with one of Enlighten's gorgeous posters as your wallpaper.

To download the free iPhone app and wallpapers, go to:
www.enlighteneducation.com/shop/

Enlighten Education on Facebook: www.facebook.com
'Like' the Enlighten Education page on Facebook to join a community of thousands of other Amazon girls and women who want to make a difference!

Enlighten Education company website:
www.enlighteneducation.com
+ We deliver in-school workshops for girls on self-esteem, body image, managing friendships, personal safety and career pathways

The Butterfly Effect:
www.enlighteneducation.edublogs.org
+ My blog, with weekly posts on hot topics related to girls

Positive self-esteem and body image

Websites

American sites providing media literacy skills needed to combat unhelpful media messages about beauty and body image:
About Face: www.about-face.org
Adios Barbie: www.adiosbarbie.com

Any Body: www.any-body.org
Love Your Body Now Foundation:
loveyourbody.nowfoundation.org
Turn Beauty Inside Out: www.tbio.org
My Pop Studio: www.mypopstudio.com

Other useful websites

Girlpower Retouch:
http://demo.fb.se/e/girlpower/retouch
+ A site that show how easy it is to distort the images we see in magazines and change someone's appearance

Jean Kilbourne: www.jeankilbourne.com
+ Writer and documentary maker who explores the way women and girls are portrayed in advertising

The Beautiful Woman Project:
www.beautifulwomenproject.org
+ American art project celebrating diversity and real, everyday beauty

Girl Guiding UK: www.girlguiding.org.uk
+ The section 'Girls Shout Out' has some particularly interesting reports on teenage mental health, active citizenship and the pressures of growing up

Kids Free 2B Kids: www.kf2bk.com
+ Australian site that raises awareness about the damage caused by the sexualisation of children and acts to combat this

Young Media Australia: www.youngmedia.org.au
+ Australian organisation with a particular interest in developing media literacy in young people

Books and magazines

New Moon Girls: American magazine aimed at 8–12-year-old girls. Has web-based activities, too: www.newmoon.com

Girl Stuff: Your full-on guide to the teen years, Kaz Cooke, Penguin, 2007

Body Talk: A power guide for girls, Elizabeth Reid Boyd and Abigail Bray, Hodder Headline, 2005

The Girlosophy series, Anthea Paul, Allen and Unwin

The Girlforce series, Nikki Goldstein, ABC Books

Friendship

Websites

Bullying No Way: www.bullyingnoway.com.au
+ Australian site that aims to develop and share frameworks for schools that work in eliminating bullying

Cyberbullying: http://yp.direct.gov.uk/cyberbullying
+ 'Laugh at it and you're part of it.' A UK site with solid tips on dealing with cyberbullying and bullying at school

Book

Respect: A girl's guide to getting respect and dealing when your line is crossed, by Courtney Macavinta and Vander Pluym, Free Spirit Publishing, 2005

Teen girls in crisis

Websites

Better Health: www.betterhealth.vic.gov.au
+ Health and medical information for consumers, quality assured by the Victorian government

Beyondblue: www.beyondblue.org.au
+ Australian website on depression

Black Dog Institute: www.blackdoginstitute.org.au
+ Australian website on depression

National Prescribing Service: www.nps.org.au
+ Consumer advice on medications; funded by the Australian Government Department of Health and Ageing

Reach Out!: www.reachout.com.au
+ Advice targeted to young people, on their mental health and wellbeing

Youthbeyondblue: www.youthbeyondblue.com
+ Australian website about young people and depression

My Body, My Life:
www.latrobe.edu.au/psy/projects/bodylife/index.html
+ A free eight-week internet-based group program for 12–18-year-old girls with a range of body-image concerns or unhealthy eating behaviours

The Butterfly Foundation:
www.thebutterflyfoundation.org.au
+ Supports Australians with eating disorders

Suicide Prevention: www.suicidepreventionaust.org
+ Public health advocates in suicide and self-harm prevention

Book

It Will Get Better: Finding Your Way through Teen Issues, Melinda Hutchings, Allen and Unwin, 2010

Alcohol

Websites

The Facts: www.thesalvos.org.au/need-help/the-facts
+ Downloadable report titled 'The Facts: Binge drinking and alcohol abuse'

A Lot 2 Lose: www.alot2lose.com
+ American public service announcements on underage drinking, produced by teen girls

Alcohol Info: www.alcoholinfo.nsw.gov.au
+ Offical NSW Government website on alcohol issues

What Are You Doing to Yourself?:
www.whatareyoudoingtoyourself.com
+ NSW Health site aimed at younger drinkers

My Nite: www.mynite.com.au
+ A NSW Police Force initiative offering advice for
  young people on a range of topics including safe
  partying

Consumerism

Websites

Commercial Free Childhood:
www.commercialfreechildhood.org
+ Excellent American site that aims to 'reclaim
  childhood from corporate marketers'

Choice: www.choice.com.au
+ Australian consumer information

Phone Choice: www.phonechoice.com.au
+ Australian site offering independent, unbiased
  information on mobile phones and phone plans

Fair Wear: www.fairwear.org.au
+ Australian group committed to working to prevent the exploitation of workers in the clothing industry

Learning

Websites

Think U Know: www.thinkuknow.org.au/kids
+ Australian site with advice on staying safe online

Safe Teens: www.safeteens.com
+ American site with advice on staying safe online

Learning Performance:
www.learningperformance.com.au
+ A national organisation that runs private sessions developing study skills. (Note: I used to have a financial relationship with this company, but I no longer do. This recommendation is genuine.)

Books

Max Your Marks, Rowena Austin and Annie Hastwell, Allen and Unwin, 2010
Surviving High School, Sharon Witt, Teen Talk Books, 2009

Entering the workforce

Websites

My Future: www.myfuture.edu.au
+ Australia's career information service

Australian Job Search: www.jobsearch.gov.au
+ Lists current job vacancies

Good Universities Guide: www.gooduniguide.com.au
+ Comprehensive information on university education and career options

Year 12 – What Next?: www.year12whatnext.gov.au
+ A guide to help Year 12 students plan their post-school education and training

Bullseye: www.deewr.gov.au/bullseye
+ School subjects you like and jobs they can lead to

Job Juice: www.jobjuice.gov.au
+ Useful site aimed at young people – covers everything from choosing a career path to writing CVs

Fair Work Ombudsman: www.fairwork.gov.au
+ Free advice and information on pay and conditions and workplace rights and responsibilities

Equal Opportunity for Women in the Workplace Authority: www.eowa.gov.au
+ Works towards achieving equal opportunity for women in the workplace; has a very good range of educational resources and tools

Australian Human Rights Commission: www.humanrights.gov.au/sex_discrimination
+ Profiles the work led by Elizabeth Broderick, the Sex Discrimination Commissioner and her Plan of Action Towards Gender Equality

Feminism

Books

Your Skirt Is Too Short: Sex, power, choice, Emily Maguire, Text Publishing, 2010
Full Frontal Feminism: A young woman's guide to why feminism matters, Jessica Valenti, Seal Press, 2007

References

1: The Battle Within

p. 17   'We don't need to change our bodies...' Wolf, Naomi, *The Beauty Myth*, Vintage, London, 1990

p. 19   'Statistics tell the story bluntly...' Byrnes, H., '68% of girls think they are not pretty enough', *The Sun-Herald*, 15 May 2005

p. 19   'A quarter of teenage girls...' Byrnes, H., '68% of girls think they are not pretty enough', *The Sun-Herald*, 15 May 2005

p. 22   'The average person sees around 75...' Young Media Australia, 'Advertising and Children – is advertising a fair game for kids?', January 2003

p. 22   'And one in every 11 commercials...' Dittrich, L., 'About-Face Facts on the Media', www.about-face.org

p. 23   'During the last three decades...' Spitzer, Brenda L., Henderson, Katherine A., Zivian, Marilyn T., 'Gender 'Differences in Population Versus Media Body Sizes: A comparison over four decades', *Sex Roles: A Journal of Research*, Vol. 40, 1999

p. 24   'What's great about this is...' *America's Next Top Model*, Bravo TV, season 8, week 4, 2007

p. 25   'And even then, "in the fickle..."' Waters, Georgia, 'Is Tahnee really our next top model?' *Brisbane Times*, www.brisbanetimes.com.au, 8 July 2009

p. 26   'She wrote: "Apart from a few notable exceptions..."' Freedman, Mia, 'Voluntary code of conduct: why I was wrong', www.mamamia.com.au, 18 May 2011

p. 28   'Health experts warn that we are...' 'Overweight and Obesity in Adults, Australia, 2004–05', Australian Bureau of Statistics, www.abs.gov.au, 25 January 2008, accessed 14 February 2009

p. 28   'Meanwhile, large numbers of us...' Byrnes, H., '68% of girls think they are not pretty enough', *The Sun-Herald*, 15 May 2005

p. 28   'Within two years, 95 per cent of people...' Healy, Justin, ed., 'Dieting and Eating Disorders', *Issues in Society*, vol. 235, www.spinneypress.com.au, 2006

p. 29   'Some recent studies have shown...' As discussed by Jenny O'Dea in 'Body Image', STATEing Women's Health Newsletter, Spring 2007, Women's Health Statewide, Children, Youth & Women's Health Service (South Australia)

p. 29   'At least one in five teen girls...' As discussed by Jenny O'Dea in 'Body Image', STATEing Women's Health Newsletter, Spring 2007, Women's Health Statewide, Children, Youth & Women's Health Service (South Australia)

p. 29   'A Victorian study of kids...' Patton, G. C., et. al., 'Adolescent Dieting: Healthy weight control or borderline eating disorder?' *Journal of Child Psychology and Psychiatry, and Allied Disciplines*, vol. 38, no. 3, 1997, pp. 299–306, available on Eating Disorders Foundation of Victoria's website, www.eatingdisorders.org.au

p. 29   'A Sydney study of children...' O'Dea, J. A. and Abraham, S., 'Food Habits, Body Image and Weight Control Practices of Young Male and Female Adolescents', *Australian Journal of Nutrition & Dietetics*, vol. 53, no. 1, 1996, available on Eating Disorders Foundation of Victoria's website, www.eatingdisorders.org.au

p. 29   'We can be well educated, creative...' Martin, Courtney E., *Perfect Girls, Starving Daughters*, Free Press, New York, 2007

p. 32   'Did you know that horse racing...' Statistic from the report 'Towards a Level Playing Field: sport and gender in Australian media, January 2008 – July 2009', Australian Sports Commission, 2010

p. 34   'A Melbourne school made news...' Gardiner, Stephanie, 'We brush, not airbrush, hair: Sydney principals say Melbourne school's photo request "silly"', *The Sydney Morning Herald*, www.smh.com.au, 6 April 2011

p. 35   'Sometimes I wish I could go back...' Montag, Heidi, interviewed by Cynthia McFadden, *Primetime: Celebrity Plastic Surgery Gone Too Far?*, ABC News, 24 November 2010

p. 37   'Researcher Karen Roberts McNamara notes...'
Roberts McNamara, Karen, 'Pretty Woman: Genital
Plastic Surgery and the Production of the Sexed Female
Subject', *gnovis*, Communication, Culture and Technology,
Georgetown University, http://gnovisjournal.org, Fall
2006

p. 37   'Hewitt told her host "Women should vajazzle..."'
Love Hewitt, Jennifer, interviewed by George Lopez, *Lopez
Tonight*, tbs, 12 January 2010

p. 38   'The producers had set out to show...' *The Sex
Education Show*, Cheetah Television for Channel 4, 2009

p. 39   'For now, the more extreme performances of feminin-
ity...' Hess, Amanda, 'The Problem with Defending the
Sacred Choice to Vajazzle', www.washingtoncitypaper.com,
15 March 2010

p. 48   'I don't want the next generation...' Kate Winslet,
quoted by Henry, L., 'Kate Winslet on Body Image', www.
suite101.com, 27 September 2006, accessed 6 February
2009

2: Beyond Generation Bratz

p. 51   'The APA reported that...' The Australian
Psychological Society's 'Submission to the Inquiry into the
sexualisation of children in the contemporary media environment', April 2008

p. 51   'The Australian Psychological Society is so concerned...' 'Helping girls develop a positive self image'

tip sheet, The Australian Psychological Society, www. psychology.org.au

p. 53   'When I was flipping through an issue ...' *Girlpower*, June 2008

p. 58   'In the results of a sex survey in *Dolly* ...' Of the readers who completed the survey, 53 per cent reportedly said they had given oral sex to a boy. *Dolly*, June 2008

p. 59   'In the 2009 UK television series *The Sex Education Show* ...' *The Sex Education Show*, Cheetah Television for Channel 4, episode 1, 2009

p. 62   'In fact, research shows that many only take part in it ...' *Australian Women's Forum*, submission to the National Council to Reduce Violence Against Women and Children, 2008

p. 63   'An extreme example would be ...' Cobb, M., 'Ambivalent Sexism and Misogynistic Rap Music: Does Exposure to Eminem Increase Sexism?', *Journal of Applied Social Psychology*, vol. 37, 2008

p. 63   'The American Academy of Pediatrics ...' These comments were made by Dr Michael Rich, spokesperson for the American Academy of Pediatrics Media Matters campaign.

p. 64   'A British study found that watching video clips ...' Bell, B. T., Lawton, R., Dittmar, H. 'The impact of thin models in music videos on adolescent girls' body dissatisfaction', *Body Image*, 2007

p. 67   'Amongst the women I know ...' Maguire, Emily,

Your Skirt Is Too Short: Sex, power, choice, Text Publishing, Melbourne, 2010, p.

p. 71   'Amanda Gordon, President of the Australian Psychological Society...', Amanda Gordon, quoted in 'Letting Kids Be Kids', *Today Tonight*, Channel 7, 29 March 2007

3: Planet Girlfriend: The Highest Highs, the Lowest Lows

p. 80   'The lyrics (that I knew for definite)...' 'Big Girls', Buckfield, Linda Mary / The Electric Pandas

p. 88   'A study by a group of Australian academics...' 'Teens subjected to mobile phone bullying', Drennan, J., Brown, M., and Sullivan-Mort, G. 'M-bullying and mobile communication: Impacts on self-esteem and well-being.' Unpublished working paper, January 2008

p. 88   'A similar study found...' Sixty-one per cent of young people said they had been bullied online. Survey by NetAlert and Ninemsn, 2009, cited in Peer Support Australia, 'Submission to the Parliament of Australia Senate Inquiry into Cyber-safety', Submission No. 48, www.aph.gov.au/house/committee/jscc/subs/sub_48.pdf

p. 89   'Teenagers' brains "are all tuned up ..."' Fuller, A. 'Into the Mystery of the Adolescent Mind', *Byron Child*, no. 16, December 2005–February 2006

p. 95   'They are based on the respect rules...' Macavint, Courtney and Vander Plimyn, Andrea, *Respect: a girl's guide to getting respect and dealing when your line is crossed*, Free Spirit Press, Minneapolis, 2005

p. 103   'A Current Affair said he had "finally ..."' McCormack, Ben (interviewer), 'Bullying Victim Speaks Out', *A Current Affair*, Nine Network, 20 March 2011

p. 104   'Teachers are of course responsible for ...' Statistic from 'Spotlight on ... Bystander Behaviour', www.bullying-noway.com.au

p. 104   'He told me that his number one ...' Patterson, Senior Constable Rob, interviewed by Dannielle Miller, 'Bullying: It's time to focus on solutions', blog post, The Butterfly Effect, www. enlighteneducation.edublogs.org, 23 March 2011

p. 106   'As a teenager, I spent many hours ...' Hansen, Rachel, 'Making Friends with Facebook: Technology has changed, but teens still just want to connect', blog post, The Butterfly Effect, www. enlighteneducation.edublogs.org, 18 November 2010

p. 107   'In fact, research by Girl Scouts USA ...' Girl Scouts of the USA, 'Who's That Girl? Image and Social Media Survey', www.girlscouts.org, 2010

4: Drinks with the Girls

p. 109   'Studies reveal that girls aged 12 to 15 ...' Cited by Harrison, D., and Gordon, J., 'Booze blitz: alcopop tax lifted by 70%', *The Age*, 27 April 2008

p. 109   'Over 80 per cent of the drinking done by children ...'

Healey, Justin (ed.), 'Alcohol Abuse', *Issues in Society*, volume 252, www.spinneypress.com.au, 2007

p. 113 'In 2008, Australian consumer group Choice...' 'Alcopops', www.choice.com.au, February 2008

p. 113 'What every girl should know about alcohol' All facts and statistics in this section are sourced from 'Women's Health' on the Australian Government's website www.therightmix.gov.au

p. 121 'As Jennifer Duncan reported...' Duncan, Jennifer, 'Binge drinking, much more than a youth issue', *The Sunday Mail*, 22 June 2008

p. 122 'Promising news came out of...' Page, Robyn, Lovett, Judy and Risbey, Sonya, 'Rethinking the drinking', St Peter's Collegiate Girl's School, Adelaide, July 2005

5: Shopping for labels . . . or love?

p. 129 'Your generation has been found...' Bachmann Achenreiner, G., & Roedder John, D., 'The meaning of brand names to children: A developmental investigation', *Journal of Consumer Psychology*, vol. 13, no. 3, 2003, quoted in 'Materialism, and Family Stress' fact sheet, Commercial Free Childhood, www.commercialfreechildhood.org

p. 129 'The average teenager in the United States...' Heim, K., 'Teen talk is, like, totally branded', *Brandweek*, 6 August 2007, quoted in 'Materialism, and Family Stress' fact sheet, Commercial Free Childhood, www.commercialfree childhood.org

p. 129   'In the UK, almost half of children...' Nairn, A., Ormrod, J., & Bottomley, P., 'Watching, wanting and well-being: exploring the links', National Consumer Council, London, 2007, quoted in 'Materialism and Family Stress' fact sheet, Commercial Free Childhood, www.commercial freechildhood.org

p. 129   'In Australia, children aged ten to 17...' Statistics compiled in YouthSCAN 2007, by Quantum Market Research, reported in 'YouthSCAN 2007', NSW Office of Fair Trading, Reviews and Reports, www.fairtrading.nsw.gov.au

p. 129   'Australian teens are working and earning more...' Statistics compiled in YouthSCAN 2007, by Quantum Market Research, reported in 'YouthSCAN 2007', NSW Office of Fair Trading, Reviews and Reports, www. fairtrading.nsw.gov.au

p. 129   'Researchers have even found...' Schor, J., *Born to Buy*, Scribner, New York, 2004, quoted in 'Materialism, and Family Stress' fact sheet, Commercial Free Childhood, www.commercialfreechildhood.org

p. 130   'Kids are the most powerful sector...' Quoted in Quart, A., *Branded: The buying and selling of teenagers*, Perseus Publishing, New York, 2003

p. 131   'At the age of five, Suri Cruise...''Glamour's Best Dressed Women 2011', *Glamour*, www.glamourmagazine.co.uk

p. 134   'Australian cosmetics guru Napoleon Perdis...' www. napoleonperdis.com

p. 134   'Jennifer Thomson wrote, "'Girl Power" is...'

Thomson, J., 'Girl Power', www.thefword.org.uk, 5 April 2008

p. 135 'And as *Glamour* ranked her number 15...' 'Glamour's Best Dressed Women 2011', *Glamour*, www.glamourmagazine.co.uk

p. 137 'While many teenagers are branded...' Quart, A., *Branded: The buying and selling of teenagers*, Perseus Publishing, New York, 2003

p. 137 'As Alissa Quart writes...' Quart, Alissa, *Branded: The buying and selling of teenagers*, Perseus Publishing, New York, 2003

p. 147 'Almost 10 per cent of people who went bankrupt. .' Australian Government Insolvency and Trust Service Australia, 'Profiles of Debtors 2007', www.itsa.gov.au, 23 September 2008

p. 147 'The highest stress level is among those...' Statistics compiled in YouthSCAN 2007, by Quantum Market Research, reported in 'YouthSCAN 2007', NSW Office of Fair Trading, Reviews and Reports, www.fairtrading.nsw.gov.au

p. 147 'A spokeswoman for the New South Wales...' 'Mobile phones "bankrupting" more teens', *The Sydney Morning Herald*, 7 November 2007

p. 150 'You may remember the story of...' 'Teen sends 14,500 texts in a month', news.ninemsn.com.au, 12 January 2009

p. 155 'What I really want that money can't buy...'

Winning entry in the 'What I really want that money can't buy' contest, Center for a New American Dream, www. newdream.org

6: Rage and Despair: Girls in Crisis

p. 158   'Girls "are in a crisis of rage..."' Straus, M. B., *Adolescent Girls in Crisis*, W. W. Norton & Company, New York, 2007

p. 158   'In fact, a book written for teen girls I read...' Witt, Sharon, *Teen Talk: Girl Talk*, Collective Wisdom Publications, Mt Evelyn, Victoria, 2008, p. 5

p. 160   'I was 12 and very reluctant to grow up...' Hansen, Rachel, 'Taking the Blues out of Puberty: Part 1', blog post, The Butterfly Effect, www.enlighteneducation.edublogs. org, 16 June 2011

p. 163   'If you could read my mind...' An eating disorder sufferer, 'Welcome to the Wasteland', blog post, The Butterfly Effect, www.enlighteneducation.edublogs.org, 23 July 2009

p. 166   'The suicide risk of a person with an eating disorder...' Statistic appears in 'Myths and Stereotypes', Eating Disorders Foundation Incorporated, www.edf.org.au

p. 167   'One study showed that 96 per cent...' Wilson, J. L., et. al., 'Surfing for Thinness: A pilot study of pro-eating disorder web site usage in adolescents with eating disorders', *Pediatrics*, vol. 118, no. 6, December 2006

p. 167   'Another study showed that these sites...' Bardone-Cone, A. M., Cass, K. M., 'What does viewing a pro-anorexia website do? An experimental examination of website exposure and moderating effects', *International Journal of Eating Disorders*, vol. 40, no. 6, 2007

p. 167 'Yet the biggest risk factor ...' According to the New South Wales Eating Disorders Foundation, 'Frequent and extreme dieting is the biggest risk factor in the development of an eating disorder,' in 'Myths and Stereotypes', Eating Disorders Foundation Incorporated, www.edf.org.au

p. 173 'Right now, between 2 and 5 per cent...' 'What is depression?', Youthbeyondblue, www.youthbeyondblue.com

p. 174 'And personality may play a role ...''Causes of depression', Black Dog Institute, www.blackdoginstitute.org.au, accessed 23 January 2009

p. 174 'If you feel that for a period of two weeks ...' Based on 'Understanding Depression', beyondblue, www.beyondblue.org.au

p. 177 'The highest rate of suicide in females ...' Based on the most recent figures available in January 2009, 'Causes of Death, Australia, 2006', Australian Bureau of Statistics, www.abs.gov.au

p. 180 'In fact, four out of five young people...''Youth suicide prevention – the warning signs', www.betterhealth.vic.gov.au

p. 183 'Heroin, cocaine and ecstasy are used by fewer...' 'Teenagers and Substance Abuse', www.healthfirst.net.au, an ACT Government initiative for the people of the Australian Capital Territory and surrounding region

p. 183 'Amphetamines, such as speed and crystal meth...' 'Teenagers and Substance Abuse', www.healthfirst.net. au, an ACT Government initiative for the people of the Australian Capital Territory and surrounding region

p. 183 'On the other hand, 25 in every hundred...' 'Teenagers and Substance Abuse', www.healthfirst.net.au, an ACT Government initiative for the people of the Australian Capital Territory and surrounding region

p. 183 'But to put the risk in perspective...' 'Australian Social Trends, 2008: Risk-taking by young people', Australian Bureau of Statistics, www.abs.gov.au, 23 July 2008

p. 185 'We know that adolescent brains...' Associate Professor Michael Baigent, quoted in 'Tackling teen drug use', beyondblue, www.beyondblue.org.au, 28 May 2007

p. 187 'As Martha Straus says...' Straus, M. B., *Adolescent Girls in Crisis*, W. W. Norton & Company, New York, 2007

7: Schooling for Life

p. 193 '[T]hose who work in and for schools...' Whitby, G., 'Pedagogies for the 21st century, having the courage to see freshly', a paper delivered at the Australian Council of Educational Leaders annual conference, 2007

p. 196 'In fact, girls outperformed boys...' Statistic from 'NSW Girls Outdo Boys in HSC', Nine News, http://news.ninemsn.com.au, 14 December 2010

p. 197 'In Australia, girls are more likely than boys...'

Statistics in this paragraph are based on 'Girls and ICT', what the research tells us', Department of Education and Training, www.schools.nsw.edu.au

p. 198   'Did you ever see the infographic...' Sass, Maria, 'Which Female Tech Influencer Are YOU? [Infographic]', The Wpromote Blog, www.wpromote.com/blog/, 20 January 2011

p. 203   'Consultant psychologist Dr Judith Paphazy...' Dr Judith Paphazy quoted in Milburn, C., 'Cotton-wool kids must burst bubble', *The Age*, 3 October 2005

p. 210   'I keep telling Dad I need a bigger monitor...' Thomas, A., *Youth Online: Identity and literacy in the digital age*, Peter Lang Publishing, 2007, as cited in Williams, B. T., 'Tomorrow Will Not Be Like Today: Literacy and Identity in a world of multiliteracies'. *Journal of Adolescent & Adult Literacy*, 51(8), May, 2008

8: Career Girl

p. 219   'On average, the weekly pay a woman...' 'Average Weekly Earnings, Australia, 2007', Australian Bureau of Statistics, reported in 'Generation f: attract, engage, retain', Equal Opportunity for Women in the Workplace Agency, www.eowa.gov.au, 2008

p. 219   'The imbalance is right there from the beginning...' *GradStats*, Graduate Careers Australia, no. 12, December 2007, reported in 'Generation f: attract, engage, retain', EOWA, www.eowa.gov.au, 2008

p. 219 'In senior levels of business...' 'EOWA Census of ASX200 Companies: Gender distribution of income for top earners', EOWA, 2006, reported in 'Generation f: attract, engage, retain', www.eowa.gov.au, 2008

p. 219 'Out of all 200 companies that make up...' 'EOWA Australian Census of Women in Leadership', EOWA, 2006, reported in 'Generation f: attract, engage, retain', www.eowa. gov.au, 2008

p. 219 'Finally, and unsurprisingly, women...' According to a 2002 study by the Human Rights and Equality Opportunity Commission, 86 per cent of reported incidents of sexual harassment involved a female victim and a male perpetrator. 'Sexual Harassment: A bad business. Review of sexual harassment in employment complaints 2002', HREOC, 2003, reported in 'Generation f: attract, engage, retain', EOWA, www.eowa.gov.au, 2008

p. 221 'In fact, the federal government's Equal Opportunity for Women in the Workplace Agency...' 'Generation f: attract, engage, retain', EOWA, www.eowa.gov.au, 2008

p. 223 'One survey showed that almost 70 per cent...' Barclay, R. G., et. al., 'Fitting Fathers into Families: Men and the fatherhood role in contemporary Australia', Department of Family and Community Services, 1999, quoted in 'Generation f: Attract, engage, retain', EOWA, www.eowa. gov.au, 2008

p. 223 'Another found that 60 per cent...' 'Striking the balance: Women, men, work and family', Sex Discrimination

Unit, HREOC, 2005, quoted in 'Generation f: attract, engage, retain', EOWA, www.eowa.gov.au, 2008

p. 224   'Women with partners spend almost 30 hours each week...' Headey, B., et. al., 'Families, Incomes and Jobs: A statistical report of the HILDA survey', Melbourne Institute of Applied Economic and Social Research, The University of Melbourne, 2006, quoted in 'Generation f: attract, engage, retain', EOWA, www.eowa.gov.au, 2008

p. 224   'While the professional and legal positions...' Maguire, E. *Princesses and Pornstars*, Text Publishing, Melbourne, 2005

p. 230   'There is nothing enlightening about shrinking...' Williamson, M., *A Return to Love*, HarperCollins, New York, 1992

p. 233   'I insisted we have a structured program ...' Freedman, M., 'Once upon a time, there was a banana', Mia Freedman blog, www.mamamia.com.au, 27 April 2008

p. 238   'Most teenagers can find only part-time work...' The unemployment rate for 15–24-year-olds is 2.8 times higher than that of 25–64-year-olds: 'How Young People are Faring '08', The Foundation for Young Australians, www.dsf.org.au, 2008

p. 240   'The 8 Employability Skills' This list is based on one compiled by the Department of Education, Science and Training, the Australian Chamber of Commerce and Industry, and the Business Council of Australia

p. 241   'Young people wanting to start their own ...' Preston,

L., *Leanne Preston and the Wild Child Story*, Random House Australia, Sydney, 2007

Every effort has been made to acknowledge and contact the copyright holders for permission to reproduce material contained in this book. Any copyright holders who have been inadvertently omitted from acknowledgements and credits should contact the publisher; omissions will be rectified in subsequent editions.

Permission to quote material from the following sources is gratefully acknowledged:

Mia Freedman, www.mamamia.com.au. Reprinted with permission.

Dannielle Miller and Melinda Tankard Reist, 'The Grinches who Steal Innocence', *The Sydney Morning Herald*, 4 January 2008.

Winning entry in the 'What I really want that money can't buy' contest, © Center for a New American Dream. Used with permission. All rights reserved.

Acknowledgements

I thank the following people with my whole heart.

In my day-to-day work:
All the teenage girls I have worked with. You shine so brightly that at times I am almost blinded by your magnificence. Love and Light to you all.

Love and healing Light, too, for the families of Paris Wilson and Cameron O'Neill-Mullin. All of us at Enlighten Education are honoured to have played a part in your daughters' last weeks.

The schools that allow me the privilege of working with their girls.

Francesca Kaoutal, my Yellow Brick Road partner who always says 'yes' and always makes me laugh.

Jane Higgins, Storm Greenhill-Brown, Diane Illingworth-Wilcox, Rachel Hansen, Nikki Davis, and Catherine Manning – my Enlighten Amazons who have not only shared the dream but have helped it grow larger and more vivid. So many of you are not only my colleagues but my family. Thank you, also, Christine Elias